When Someone Dies
IN NEW YORK

ALL THE LEGAL AND PRACTICAL THINGS
YOU NEED TO DO
WHEN SOMEONE NEAR TO YOU DIES
IN THE STATE OF NEW YORK

By AMELIA E. POHL, Attorney at Law

with New York attorney
VINCENT J. RUSSO
as consulting counsel

and
BARBARA J. SIMMONDS, Ph.D.
as consulting psychologist

 EAGLE PUBLISHING COMPANY OF BOCA

Copyright © 2000 by AMELIA E. POHL
All rights reserved.

No part of this book may be reproduced or transmitted for any purpose, in any form and by any means, graphic, electronic or mechanical, including photocopying, recording, or by any information storage or retrieval system, without permission in writing from AMELIA E. POHL.

The purpose of this book is to provide the reader with an accurate and informative overview of the subject but laws change frequently and are subject to different interpretations as courts rule on the meaning or effect of a law. This book is sold with the understanding that neither the publisher nor the authors are engaging in, nor rendering legal, medical, psychiatric, accounting or any other professional service. If you need legal, accounting, medical, psychiatric or other expert advice, then you should seek the services of a duly licensed professional.

WEB SITES: Web sites appear throughout the book. These Web sites are offered for the convenience of the reader only. Publication of these Web site addresses is not an endorsement by the authors, editors or publishers of this book.

This book is intended for use by the consumer for his or her own benefit. If you use this book to counsel someone about the law, accounting or medicine, then that may be considered an unauthorized and illegal practice.

EAGLE PUBLISHING COMPANY OF BOCA
4199 N. Dixie Highway, #2
Boca Raton, FL   33431
E-mail   eagleonline@attglobal.net

Printed in the United States of America
ISBN   1-892407-10-8
Library of Congress Catalog Card Number: 99-69963

About the Author

Before becoming an attorney in 1985, AMELIA E. POHL taught mathematics on both the high school and college level. During her tenure as Associate Professor of Mathematics at Prince George's Community College in Maryland, she wrote several books including Probability: A Set Theory Approach, Principals of Counting and Common Stock Sense.

During her practice of law Attorney Pohl observed that many people want to reduce the high cost of legal fees by performing or assisting with their own legal transactions. Attorney Pohl found that, with a bit of guidance, people are able to perform many legal transactions for themselves. Attorney Pohl is utilizing her background as teacher, author and attorney to provide that "bit of guidance" to the general public in the form of self-help legal books that she has written. Attorney Pohl is currently working on "translating" this book for the rest of the 49 states:

When Someone Dies In Arkansas

When Someone Dies in Connecticut, etc.

Consulting New York Attorney

VINCENT J. RUSSO is nationally recognized for his contribution and achievements in the field of Elder Law. He is the Managing and Founding Shareholder of Vincent J. Russo & Associates, P.C. with offices in Westbury and Islandia, New York. As a noted authority, author and lecturer in Elder Law, Mr. Russo has championed the rights of the elderly since 1985. He is also certified in Elder Law by the National Elder Law Foundation.

Mr. Russo helped launch the practice of Elder Law as a Founding Member of the National Academy of Elder Law Attorneys, of which he is a Past President and Fellow. He brought the success of his achievement to the New York State Bar Association and is a Founding Member and Past Chair of its Elder Law Section.

Mr. Russo earned his law degree from Fordham University School of Law and a Masters of Law in Taxation from the Boston University of Law. He is admitted to the New York, Massachusetts and Florida State Bar Associations, and is a Co-Author of New York Elder Law Practice (for professionals) published by the West Group. You can visit Mr. Russo's web site at http://www.russoelderlaw.com.

Consulting Psychologist

BARBARA J. SIMMONDS, Ph.D., a noted psychologist, has collaborated with the author on those sections of this book dealing with the grieving process. Dr. Simmonds has been practicing in the field of Health/Rehabilitation Psychology and Gerontology for the past 10 years. Her experiences in the field led her as a natural outcome to develop expertise also in Grief Counseling, since so many losses accrue to individuals in a health care setting.

In addition to her work in hospitals, nursing centers and private practice, Dr. Simmonds has served as Adjunct Faculty at Nova Southeastern University, teaching courses in Aging, Stress Management and Grief Counseling. Dr. Simmonds holds a Master's Degree in Gerontology and a Ph.D. in Clinical Psychology from Nova Southeastern University. She was the Director of Psychological Services at Villa Maria Nursing and Rehabilitation Center for eight years and now continues her relationship with the institution on a consultation basis. She continues with her private practice in North Miami, Florida.

To my brother, Paul Adinolfi,
his intelligence, good humor and kindness,
his strength during our times of family loss,
have set the beacon standard for me to follow.

ACKNOWLEDGMENTS

When someone dies, the family attorney is often among the first to be called. Family members have questions about whether probate is necessary, who to notify, how to get possession of the assets, etc. Over the years, as we practiced in the field of Elder Law, we noticed that the questions raised were much the same family to family. We both agreed that a book answering such questions would be of service to the general public. We wish to thank all of the clients, whom we have had the honor and pleasure to serve, for providing us with the impetus to produce this book.

Special thanks from AMELIA E. POHL
I wish to express my sincere appreciation for the assistance and encouragement given to me by Dominick Martiniello, Susann Martiniello, Michael J. DeMarie, CPA, my daughters Louise Lucas and Margot Bosche, and to my husband J. William Pohl.

Special thanks from VINCENT J. RUSSO
To my partner Marie Elena Puma, for her assistance in ensuring that the latest New York laws and estate administrative practices are reflected in this book. Thanks to my associates, Wendy H. Sheinberg, Jane E. Bernstein and Charles E. Baron for the statutory and case cites and to my assistants, Kelley Martinez and Julie Lucisano, for their help.

My gratitude to Marvin Rachlin who has been my mentor, and to my wife, Susan, and my children, Dante, Lizzy and Robert for "standing by me" and Theresa for always looking over my shoulder.

When Someone Dies in New York

CONTENTS

About this book

We have tried to make this book as comprehensive as possible so there are specialized sections of the book that do not apply to the general population and may not be of interest to you. The following GUIDE POSTS appear throughout the book. You can read the section if the situation applies to you or skip the section if it doesn't.

GUIDE POSTS

The SPOUSE POST means that the information provided is specifically for the spouse of the decedent. If the decedent was single, then skip this section.

The CALL-A-LAWYER POST alerts you to a situation that may require the assistance of an attorney. See page xiii for suggestions about how to find a lawyer.

The CAUTION POST alerts you to a potential problem. It is followed by a suggestion about how to avoid the problem.

The SPECIAL SITUATION POST means that the information given in that paragraph applies to a particular event or situation; for example when the decedent dies a violent death. If the situation does not apply in your case, then you can skip the section.

The Organization of the Book

There are six steps in settling the decedent's estate:

1. Tending to the funeral and burial
2. Telling everyone that the person died
3. Locating all of the decedent's property
4. Paying any outstanding bills
5. Determining who are the beneficiaries
6. Getting the decedent's property to the proper beneficiary

We devoted a chapter to each of these 6 steps. We placed a CHECK LIST at the end of Chapter 6 to assist you in organizing the many things that need to be done.

Chapters 1 through 6 identify problems that can occur when someone dies. Chapters 7 and 8 explain how to set up your own estate plan so that your family is not burdened by similar problems. Chapter 9 offers suggestions that may help if you are having difficulty getting through the grieving process.

GLOSSARY

This book is designed for the average reader. Legal terminology has been kept to a minimum. There is a glossary at the end of the book in the event you come across a legal term that is not familiar to you.

FICTITIOUS NAMES AND EVENTS

The examples in this book are based loosely on actual events; however, all names are fictitious and the events as portrayed, are fictitious.

Reading the Law

Where applicable, we identified the state statute or federal statute that is the basis of the discussion. We did this as a reference, and also to encourage the general public to read the law as it is written. Prior to the Internet the only way you could look up the law was to physically take yourself to the local courthouse law library or the law section of a public library. Today all of the state and federal statutes are literally at your finger tips. They are just a mouse click away on the Internet. All you need to look up the law is the address of the web site and the identifying number of the statute:

NEW YORK STATUTE WEB SITE
http://assembly.state.ny.us/ALIS
FEDERAL STATUTE WEB SITE
http://www4.law.cornell.edu/uscode

New York has consolidated their laws into 111 titles that are listed alphabetically. Each title is divided into numbered sections. For example:
(Surrogate's 1750) refers to Section 1750 of the Surrogate's Court Procedure Act.

(Estates 3-1.1) refers to Section 3-1.1 of the Estates, Powers & Trusts laws.

To look up a statute, all you need do is go to the web site, find the title and then the section within the title.

If you come across a topic that is of importance to you, then you may find it both interesting and profitable to actually read the law as written.

When You Need A Lawyer

This book describes New York law as in effect when the book was written. We pay our legislators (state and federal) to make laws and, if necessary, change those in effect. We pay judges to interpret the law and that interpretation may change the way the law operates. The legislature and the judiciary do their job and so laws change frequently.

The purpose of the book is to give the reader an overview of what needs to be done when someone dies, and to provide information about how a person can arrange his own affairs to avoid problems for his own family. It is not intended as a substitute for legal counsel or any other kind of professional advice. If you have any legal question, then you should seek the counsel of an attorney. When looking for an attorney, consider three things:
EXPERTISE, COST and PERSONALITY.

EXPERTISE

The state of New York does not have a program to certify that an attorney is specialized in a particular area of law. An attorney in New York may represent to the public that he/she is a certified specialist in a given area of law if the attorney is certified by an organization recognized by New York State. For example, the National Elder Law Foundation has a certification program for the field of Elder Law. An attorney certified by the Foundation, is allowed to make that fact known to the public. Also, attorneys are allowed to state that they limit their practice to a certain kind of law or that they are experienced in an area of law. Before employing an attorney for a job, ask how long he/she has practiced that type of law and what percentage of the practice is devoted to that type of law.

You can call the New York State Bar Association's Lawyer Referral and Information Service at (800)342-3661 for a referral to an attorney who is experienced in the field of law that your seek.

Of course, the best way to find an attorney is through personal referral. Ask your friends, family or business acquaintances if they have used an attorney for the field of law that you seek and whether they were pleased with the results. It is important to employ an attorney who is experienced in the kind of law you seek. Your friend may have a wonderful Estate Planning attorney, but if you have suffered an injury, then you need a Personal Injury attorney.

COST

In addition to the attorney's experience, it is important that you check out what you can expect to pay in attorney's fees. When you call for an appointment ask what the attorney will charge for the initial consultation and the approximate cost for the service you seek. Ask whether there will be any additional costs such as filing fees, accounting fees, expert witness fees, etc.

If the least expensive attorney is out of your price range then there are many state and private agencies throughout the state that provide legal assistance for people of low income. You can look up the nearest Legal Service in your telephone directory, or you can call the local Bar Association for the telephone number of the local Pro Bono Organization. The American Bar Association has a web site that lists telephone numbers for New York state Pro Bono Programs:

THE AMERICAN BAR ASSOCIATION WEB SITE
http://www.abanet.org/legalservices/probono/pb-newyork.html

PERSONALITY

Of equal importance to the attorney's experience and legal fees, is your relationship with the attorney. How easy was it to reach the attorney? Did you go through layers of receptionists and legal assistants before being allowed to speak to the attorney? Did the attorney promptly return your call? If you had difficulty reaching the attorney, then you can expect similar problems should you employ that attorney.

Did the attorney treat you with respect? Did the attorney treat you paternally with a "father knows best" attitude or did the attorney treat you as an intelligent person with the ability to understand the options available to you and the ability to make your own decision based on the information provided to you.

Are you able to understand and easily communicate with the attorney? Is he/she speaking to you in plain English or is his/her explanation of the matter so full of legalese to be almost meaningless to you?

Do you find the attorney's personality to be pleasant or grating? Sometimes people rub each other the wrong way. It is like rubbing a cat the wrong way. Stroking a cat from head to tail is pleasing to the cat, but petting it in the opposite direction, no matter how well intended, causes friction. If the lawyer makes you feel annoyed or uncomfortable, then find another attorney.

It is worth the effort to take the time to interview as many attorneys as it takes to find one with the right expertise, fee schedule and personality for you.

The First Week 1

Dealing with the death of a close family member or friend is difficult. Not only do you need to deal with your own emotions, but often with those of your family and friends. Sometimes their sorrow is more painful to you, than what you are experiencing yourself.

In addition to the emotional impact of a death, there are many things that need to be done, from arranging the funeral and burial, to closing out the business affairs of the decedent, and finally giving whatever property is left to the proper beneficiary.

The funeral and burial take only a few days. Wrapping up the affairs of the decedent may take considerably longer. This chapter explains what things you (the spouse or closest family member) need to do during the first week, beginning at the moment of death and continuing through the funeral.

 MALE GENDER USED

Rather than use "he/she" or "his/her" for simplicity
(and hoping not to offend anyone)
we will refer to the decedent using the male gender.

References to other people will be in both genders.

AUTOPSIES

Years ago people died natural deaths from unknown causes. Doctors often requested permission to perform an autopsy to determine the cause of death. In today's high tech world of medicine, doctors are fairly certain of the cause of death, but if there is a question, the family may be asked permission to perform an autopsy. If, during his lifetime, the decedent appointed a Health Care Agent (someone to make his medical decisions) then the Agent must agree, in writing, to the autopsy. If no Agent was appointed, then the spouse or next of kin may give consent. If a relative or friend objects to the procedure because it is against the religious belief of the decedent, then no autopsy may be performed.
(Public Health 4210).

The cost of an autopsy runs anywhere from $2,500 to $3,500. The person giving authorization must agree to pay for the autopsy because the cost is not covered under most health insurance plans. It is in the family's best interest to consent to the autopsy because such examination might reveal a genetic disorder, that could be treated if it later appears in another family member. Even if no such disease is found, knowing the cause of death with certainty is better than not knowing.

An example that comes to mind is a woman who was taken to the hospital complaining of stomach pains. The doctors thought she might be suffering from gallbladder disease but she died before they could effectively treat her. A doctor suggested that an autopsy be performed to determine the actual cause of death. The woman had three daughters, one of whom objected to the autopsy "Why spend that kind of money?
It won't bring Mom back."

The daughter's wishes were respected and no family member consented to the procedure. However, over the years, as each of the daughters aged and became ill with their own various ailments they would undergo physical examinations. As part of taking their medical history, doctors would routinely ask "And what was cause of your mother's death?" None could answer the question.

This is not a dramatic story. No mysterious genetic disorder ever occurred in any of her daughters, nor in any of their children. But each daughter (including the one who objected) at some point in her life, was confronted with the nagging question "What did Mom die of?"

MANDATORY AUTOPSIES

When a person dies, a physician must sign the death certificate stating the cause of death. If a person dies in a hospital, then there is a doctor present to sign the certificate. If a person dies at home from natural causes or any other reason (accident, violence, suicide), then the police must be notified. The person who discovers the body should call 911 to summon the police. The police will ask the coroner or medical examiner to determine the cause of death. If there is a suspicion that the death was not from natural causes or if the decedent died from a disease that might pose a threat to the public health, then the coroner or medical examiner may, at the cost of the county, have an autopsy performed. (County 674 (3a)).

AUTOPSIES PERFORMED BY THE INSURANCE COMPANY:

A company that issues an accident or health insurance policy in New York is required to include a statement in the policy that the company has the right to perform an autopsy (Insurance 3216(c)(14d)). The cost of the autopsy must be paid for by the insurance company, so they will not order an autopsy unless there is some important reason to do so.

ANATOMICAL GIFTS

If, before death, the decedent made an anatomical gift by signing a donor card, then hospital personnel or the donor's doctor needs to be made aware of the gift in quick proximity to the time of death — preferably before death.

GIFT AUTHORIZED BY THE FAMILY

Hospital personnel determine whether a mortally ill patient is a candidate for an organ donation. Early on in the donor program those over 65 were not considered as suitable candidates. Today, however, the condition of the organ, and not the age, is the determining factor.

The federal government has established regional Organ Procurement Organizations throughout the United States to coordinate the donor program. There are Organ Procurement Organizations located in Albany (Center for Donation and Transplant), Rochester (University of Rochester OPO), New York City (New York Organ Donor Network) and Buffalo (Upstate New York Transplant Services, Inc.). If it is decided that the patient is a candidate, the hospital will contact the local Organ Procurement Organization.

The Organ Procurement Organization will determine whether the patient is a suitable donor. If they decide to request the gift and the candidate did not sign a donor card, then someone in the family must give written permission. Someone who is specially trained will approach the family to request the donation. New York statute (Public Health 4351 (4)) establishes an order of priority to authorize the donation: 1st   spouse

2nd   son or daughter who is 18 or older
3rd   either parent
4th   brother or sister who is 18 or older
5th   guardian who was appointed before death

If permission is obtained from a family member and there are others in the same or a higher priority, then an effort must be made to contact those people and make them aware of the proposed gift. For example, if the sister of the decedent agrees to the gift (4th in priority) and the decedent had an adult child (2nd in priority), then the child needs to be made aware of the gift. If the child objects, then no gift can be made. Similarly, the statute prohibits the gift if the decedent ever expressed his opposition to a donation.

AFTER THE DONATION

If the family agrees to the donation, then once the operation is complete the body is delivered to the funeral home and prepared for burial or cremation as directed by the family. The operation does not disfigure the body so there can be an open casket viewing if the family so wishes.

Once the donation is made, the Organ Procurement Organization keeps in touch with the donor's family. If the family wishes they will provide them with basic demographic information about the donation, such as the age, sex, marital status, number of children and occupation of the recipient of the gift.

If the recipient of the gift wishes to write to the donor's family to thank them for the gift, the Organ Procurement Organization will contact the donor's family and ask if they wish to receive the letter. If not, then the letter is kept on file in the event that the donor's family may want to read it at a later date.

GIFT FOR EDUCATION OR RESEARCH

If the decedent signed a donor card indicating his wish to use his body for any purpose and he is not a candidate for an organ donation, then you can offer to release the body to a school of medicine at a university for the purpose of education or research. Some schools that accept donations are as follows:

State University of New York   (315) 464-5120
Upstate Medical Center; Dept. of Anatomy
Syracuse, NY 13210

University of Rochester   (716) 275-2592
School of Medicine, Department of Anatomy
Rochester, NY 14642

State University of NY at Stony Brook   (631) 444-3111
Health Science Center; Dept. of Anatomical Sciences
Stony Brook, NY 11794

Cornell University Medical College   (212) 746-6140
Dept. of Anatomy and Cell Biology
New York, NY 10021

You will need to call the school within 24 hours of the death to determine whether they will accept the body. Most schools will not accept bodies from those who have died from a contagious disease or from crushing injuries or if he decedent was seriously obese. There is no charge to the family to make the donation. If the body is local to the area, the school will pay the cost of having have the body transported to the university.

New York state law requires that a licensed funeral director transport a body. The funeral director must also obtain the burial permit, copy of death certificate, and a "Release of Remains" permission statement from the next of kin. These forms need to accompany the donated body so you will need to employ a funeral director to make the transfer (Public Health 4142 and 4144).

The study takes 1 to 2 years to complete. Once the study is finished, the remains are cremated and the *cremains* (cremated remains) returned to the family. If the family wishes, the school will arrange to have the cremains scattered at sea or placed in a local cemetery depending on the current practice of the school.

THE FUNERAL

Approximately one third of the population dies suddenly from an accident or undetected illness. Two thirds of the population die after being ill for a year or more with the most common scenario being that of an aged person dying after being ill for several months. In such cases, the death is expected. Family and friends are emotionally prepared for the happening. Whether expected or unexpected, the first job is the disposition of the body.

THE PRE-ARRANGED FUNERAL

Increasingly, people are making advance arrangements for their own funeral and burial. This makes it easier on the family both financially and emotionally. All decisions have been made and there is no guessing what the decedent would have wanted.

If the decedent made provision for his burial space, then you need to locate the burial certificate. If the decedent purchased a pre-need funeral plan, then you need to locate the contract. You should read the contract to determine what provisions were made. Some contracts are paid on an installment basis. If the decedent signed such a contract, then you need to find out what monies were paid and whether there is a remaining balance due.

If you cannot locate the contract, but you know the name of the funeral home, then call and ask them to send you a copy of the contract. If you believe the decedent purchased a funeral plan but you do not know the name of the funeral home, then call the local funeral homes. Many local funeral homes are owned by national firms with computer capacity to identify people who have purchased a contract in any of their many locations.

Once you have possession of the contract, bring it with you to the funeral home and go over the terms of the contract with the funeral director. Inquire whether there is any charge that is not included in the contract.

MAKING FUNERAL ARRANGEMENTS

If the decedent died unexpectedly or without having made any prior funeral arrangements, then your first job is to choose a funeral director and make arrangements for the funeral or cremation. Most people choose the nearest or most conveniently located funeral home without comparison shopping, however prices for these services can vary significantly from funeral home to funeral home. Savings can be had if you take the time to make a few phone calls.

Receiving price quotes by telephone is your right under Federal law. Federal Trade Commission ("FTC") Rule 453.2 (b) (1) requires a funeral director to give an accurate telephone quote of the prices of his goods and services. Funeral homes are listed in the telephone directory under FUNERAL DIRECTORS. If you live in a small town, there may be only one or two listings. If such is the case, then check out some funeral homes in the next largest city.

Funeral Directors usually provide the following services:
➤ arrange for the transportation of the body
   to the funeral home and then to the burial site
➤ arrange for the embalming or cremation of the body
➤ arrange funeral and memorial services
➤ file the death certificate and order copies for the family
➤ have memorial and acknowledgment cards printed
➤ arrange to print the obituary

To compare prices you will need to determine:
- ✧ what is included in the price of a basic funeral plan
- ✧ whether you can expect any additional cost.

Embalming is necessary if you are going to have a viewing. Embalming is not necessary if you order a direct cremation or an immediate burial. Federal Trade Commission Rule 453.5 prohibits the funeral home from charging an embalming fee unless you order the service.

If the decedent did not own a burial space, then that cost must be included when making funeral arrangements.

PURCHASING THE CASKET

When comparison-shopping, you will find that the single most expensive item in the funeral arrangement is the casket.   Most funeral directors will quote you a price for the basic funeral plan. That plan does not include the cost of the casket. Directors usually quote a range of prices for the casket, saying that you will need to come in and choose the casket at the time you contract for the funeral.

When selecting a casket you should be aware that there is often a considerable markup in the price quoted by the funeral director.   You do not need to deal "sole source" in the purchase of the casket. You can purchase a casket elsewhere and have it delivered to the funeral home for use instead of the one offered by the funeral director.

In 1994, The Federal Trade Commission ruled that funeral homes had to accept caskets purchased elsewhere. (FTC Rule 453.4).   The ruling includes a ban on funeral homes charging a handling fee for accepting a casket purchased elsewhere.

If you wish to shop for a casket, then the best time to do so is before you go to the funeral home to arrange for the funeral. You can find a retail casket sales outlet in the telephone book under CASKETS. You may need to look in the telephone directory for the nearest large city to find a listing. For users of the Internet, you can use your search engine to find the retail sales casket company nearest you. By making a call to a retail casket sales dealer, you will become knowledgeable in the price range of caskets. You can then decide what is a reasonable price for the product you seek.

Once you have determined what you should pay for the casket, it is only fair to give the funeral director the opportunity to meet that price. If you cannot reach a meeting of the minds, then you can always order the casket from the retail sales dealer and have it delivered to the funeral home.

THE CREMATION

Increasingly people are opting for cremation. The reasons for choosing cremation are varied, but for the majority, it is a matter of finances. The cost of cremation is approximately one-sixth that of an ordinary funeral and burial. A major saving is the cost of the casket. No casket is necessary for the cremation. Federal law prohibits a Funeral Director from saying that a casket is required for a direct cremation (FTC Rule 453.3 (b)ii). Of course if you want to have a viewing of the body and/or a funeral service with the body present, then you may need to purchase a disposable casket made of wood or cardboard, or you can rent a casket from the Funeral Director.

If you are having a memorial service in a place of worship with no viewing of the body before the cremation, then consider contracting with a facility that does cremations only. Look in the telephone book CREMATION SERVICES. You will also see cremation "societies" in the telephone book. Some are for-profit and others non-profit. You can also find advertisements for cremation services on the Internet.

These cremation facilities provide much the same services as a funeral home but with one important exception — the cremation service does not provide any type of funeral service or public viewing of the body.

| Special Situation | THE OVERWEIGHT DECEDENT |

If the decedent weighs more than 300 pounds, then you need to check to see if the Cremation service has facilities large enough to handle the body. If you cannot locate a crematory that can accommodate the body, then you need to make burial arrangements.

DISPOSING OF THE CREMAINS

The decedent's cremains can be place in a cemetery. Many cemeteries have a separate building called a *columbarium*, which is a building especially designed to store urns. If not, then the cremains can be placed in a cemetery plot. Some cemeteries allow the cremains of a family member to to be placed in a occupied family plot. Similarly, some cemeteries will allow the cremains to be place in the space in a mausoleum that is currently occupied by a member of the decedent's family. If it is your desire to have the cremains placed in an occupied family plot or mausoleum, then you need to call the cemetery and ask them to explain their policy as it relates to the burial of urns in occupied sites.

If the cremains are to be placed in a cemetery, then you need to obtain a suitable urn for the burial. You can purchase the urn from the Funeral Director or Crematory Service Director. Urns cost much less than caskets, but they can cost several hundred dollars. You may wish to do some comparison shopping by calling a retail sales casket dealer.

The decedent may have expressed a desire that his ashes be spread out to sea. The Funeral Director or Cremation Service Director can assist you with such arrangements.

If the decedent is to be buried in another state, then the body will need to be transported to that state. Most funeral firms belong to a national network of funeral firms, and the out-of-state funeral director has the means to make local arrangements to ship the body. Contact the out-of-state funeral director and have him/her make arrangement with the airline for the transportation of the body.

If services are to be held in New York and in another state, then contact the local funeral firm and they will make arrangements with the out-of-state funeral firm to transport the body.

If the body has been cremated, then you can transport the ashes yourself, either by carrying the ashes as part of your luggage or by arranging with the airline to transport the ashes as cargo. You should have a certified copy of the death certificate available in the event that you need to identify the remains of the decedent. Call the airline before departure and ask whether they have any special regulation or procedure regarding the transportation of human ashes.

SPOUSE ▸ THE MILITARY BURIAL

Subject to availability of burial spaces, an honorably discharged veteran and/or his unmarried minor or handicapped child and/or his unremarried spouse may be buried in a national military cemetery. Some cemeteries have room only for cremated remains or for the casketed remains of a family member of someone who is currently buried in that cemetery, so you need to call to determine if there is space available.

There are four national military cemeteries in New York:

Calverton National Cemetery   (631) 727-5410
210 Princton Boulevard; Calverton, NY 11933-1031

Cypress Hills National Cemetery   (718) 277-2900
625 Jamaica Avenue; Brooklyn, NY   11208

Long Island National Cemetery   (631) 454-4949
2040 Wellwood Avenue; Farmingdale, NY 11735

Woodlawn National Cemetery   (607) 732-5411
1825 Davis Street; Elmira, NY 14901

The Department of the Army is in charge of the Arlington National Cemetery. If you wish to have an eligible deceased veteran buried in the Arlington National Cemetery, then call them at (703) 695-3250.

Arlington National Cemetery
Interment Service Branch
Arlington, VA 22211

Burial space in a National Cemetery is free of charge. Cemetery employees will open and close the grave and mark it with headstone or grave marker without cost to the family. The local Veteran's Administration ("VA") will provide the family with a memorial flag.

If the decedent was receiving a VA pension, then the VA will pay a burial and funeral expense allowance regardless of where the veteran is buried. The VA will not reimburse any burial or funeral cost for the spouse of a veteran.

For information about reimbursement of funeral and burial expenses you can call the VA at 1-800-827-1000.

The Department of Veteran's Affairs has a web site with information on the following topics:

> ➤ National and Military Cemeteries
> ➤ Burial, Headstones and Markers
> ➤ State Cemetery Grants Program
> ➤ Obtaining Military Records
> ➤ Locating Veterans

VA WEB SITE
http://www.cem.va.gov

BENEFITS FOR SPOUSE OF DECEDENT VETERAN

SPOUSE

If the decedent was honorably discharged, then regardless of where he is buried, his spouse might be eligible for a contribution from the Veteran's Administration for his funeral and burial expenses. If the decedent had minor or disabled children, his spouse may also be eligible for a monthly benefit of Dependency and Indemnity Compensation ("DIC").

If the Veteran's surviving spouse receives nursing home care under Medicaid, then the spouse might be eligible for a monthly payment from the VA. Whether the surviving spouse is eligible for any of these benefits depends on many factors including whether the decedent was serving on active duty, whether his death was service related, and the surviving spouse's assets and income.

For information about whether the surviving spouse is eligible for any benefit related to the decedent's military service, call the VETERANS ADMINISTRATION at 1-800-827-1000.

You can receive a printed statement of public policy: VA Pamphlet 051-000-00217-2 FEDERAL BENEFITS FOR VETERANS AND DEPENDENTS by sending a check in the amount of $5 to THE SUPERINTENDENT OF DOCUMENTS
P.O. Box 371954
Pittsburgh, PA 15250-7954
Information is also available on the VA web site:

VA WEB SITE
http://www.va.gov

| Special Situation | THE PROBLEM FUNERAL OR BURIAL |

The funeral and burial industry is well regulated by both state and federal government. Under New York statue (Public Health 3450), the following acts are subject to disciplinary action:

⊠ Delivering goods of a lesser quality than presented to the customer as a sample

⊠ Using a false or misleading advertisement

⊠ Paying kickbacks to generate business

⊠ Being a habitual drunkard or addicted to drugs such as morphine, opium or cocaine

Funeral directors are licensed professionals so it is unusual to have a problem with the funeral or burial or cremation. If, however, you had a bad experience with any aspect of the funeral, then you can call the state licensing agency at (518) 402-0785, or write to them: Bureau of Funeral Directing
New York State Department of Health
Empire State Plaza, Corning Tower
Albany, NY 12237-0681

If your complaint has to do with the burial, then call the state consumer protection agency of the New York State Division of Cemeteries at (518) 474-6226. Or you can write to them:
New York State Division of Cemeteries
162 Washington Avenue
Albany, NY 12231

If you are not satisfied with the results obtained, then consult with an attorney who is experienced in litigation matters.

If an indigent person dies and the police are able to identify him, they will try to locate his family. If the decedent was an honorably discharged veteran, then the Veteran's Administration will arrange for a burial. If the indigent decedent is not an honorably discharged veteran, then his family is given 24 hours to claim the body. If the family is unable or unwilling to make burial arrangements, then the person in charge of the body (hospital administrator, medical examiner, funeral director, etc.) will deliver the body to a New York medical school for the purpose of medical science and study (Public Health 4211).

If, before he died, the indigent or unidentified decedent asked that his body be buried, or if the decedent was carrying an identification card that indicates his opposition to the dissection or autopsy of his body, then those wishes are respected, and the county will arrange for the burial (Public Health 4211 (3b).

DECEASED RECIPIENT OF PUBLIC ASSISTANCE

If a person, who was receiving Public Assistance (including Title XVI Social Security Income benefits) dies without funds to bury him, the Public Welfare official will require his spouse, or if he was under 21, his parent or stepparent, to pay for the burial. If the spouse or parent has insufficient monies to do so, then the official will arrange for the burial. (Social Services 101 and 141).

If the decedent died a violent death or under circumstances in which foul play is suspected, the Medical Examiner will take possession of the body. The body will not be released to the funeral director until the examination of the body is complete. In the interim, the family can proceed with arrangements for the funeral. The funeral director will contact the Medical Examiner to determine when he can pick up the body and proceed with the funeral.

If the decedent died because of a criminal act and you are a family member, then you may wish to contact an attorney experienced in Criminal Law to learn of your rights as a family member. If the perpetrator of the crime has significant funds, you may want to sue him/her for wrongful death.

 LAWYER   THE ACCIDENTAL DEATH

If the decedent died because of an accident, then it is important to contact a Personal Injury attorney to determine whether the family has a case for wrongful death. If the accident was related to the decedent's job, the family may wish to consult with a Worker's Compensation attorney as well.

| Special Situation | THE CRIMINAL DEATH |

The New York CRIME VICTIMS SERVICE PROGRAMS provide assistance to victims of crime and their family members. The term "family member" includes anyone living in the same home with the victim or maintaining a sexual relationship with the victim. As part of the program, the state may pay for out-of-pocket losses that are not reimbursable from any other source. Such out-of-pocket losses may include medical and burial expenses and psychological counseling for family members of the victim. To be eligible for compensation:

➤ the crime must be promptly reported to authorities — at least within a week of the discovery of the crime, unless there is good cause for the delay;

➤ Application for compensation was filed within one year from the injury or death.

If the decedent died as a result of a crime, a family member can apply for compensation. Application forms are available at any New York police station or precinct house. The application for compensation must be filed with the CRIME VICTIMS' BOARD within one year of the date of the crime. The Board will conduct a hearing to determine the amount of the award. The applicant has the right to be represented by an attorney before the Board and the Board can compensate up to $1,000 of those attorney's fees. The award process may take several weeks, but if the Board determines that emergency funds are needed (for example, to pay for the burial) then the Board can release up to $1,500. Any emergency funds given will be deducted from the final award (Executive 621(4), 622, 625, 625(a), 626, 630, 631, 631(a)).

☎ LAWYER | THE MISSING BODY

Few things are more difficult to deal with than a missing person. The emotional turmoil created by the "not knowing" is often more difficult than the finality of death. The legal problems created by the disappearance are also more difficult than if the person simply died. It may take a two-part legal process — a Temporary Administration to handle the missing person's affairs while he is missing and then a final probate procedure if he is later declared dead or found dead:

APPOINTING A TEMPORARY ADMINISTRATOR

If a person is missing and cannot be found after a diligent search, then that person is referred to as an *absentee*. If the absentee has business matters that need attending (bills that need to be paid, checks that need to be cashed, etc.), then someone, a *Temporary Administrator,* will be appointed by the Surrogate's court to take charge of the missing person's property and manage it until the person can be found (Surrogate's 901). You will need to employ an attorney who is experienced in probate matters to get a Temporary Administrator appointed.

BEGINNING THE PROBATE PROCEDURE

If the circumstances of the disappearance are sufficient to justify the belief that the missing person is dead or after 5 years have passed, whichever is earlier, then the judge will issue a decree declaring the missing person to be dead. If a probate procedure is necessary, then the attorney can begin to probate the estate as soon as the absentee is declared to be dead (Surrogate's 1407 (3)).

THE DEATH CERTIFICATE

The Funeral Director or Cremation Service Director will order as many death certificates as you request. Most establishments require an original certified copy and not a photocopy so you need to order sufficient certified copies.

The following is a list of institutions that may want a certified copy:

* Each insurance company that insured the decedent or his property (health insurance company, life insurance company, car insurance company, home insurance company)

* Each financial institution in which the decedent had money invested (brokerage houses, banks)

* The decedent's pension fund

* Each credit card company used by the decedent

* The IRS

* The Social Security Administration

* The Clerk's office in each county where the decedent owned real property.

* If probate is necessary, then the Clerk of the Surrogate's court.

Some airlines and car rental companies offer a discount for short notice, emergency trips. If you have family flying in for the funeral, you may wish to order a few extra copies of the death certificate so that they can obtain an airline or car rental discount.

ORDERING COPIES OF THE DEATH CERTIFICATE

If you wish to order certified copies of the death certificate at a later date, you can call the funeral director and ask him to do so or you can order copies yourself:

FOR NEW YORK CITY:
OFFICE OF VITAL RECORDS
125 Worth Street, Box 4, Room 133
New York, NY   10013
Telephone (212) 788-4520   Fax: (800) 908-9146

You can apply for a certified copy of the death certificate by mail, telephone, fax or in person if you happen to be in Manhattan. If you want to apply by mail or fax, then it is important to first call so that you will know what information they require.

The current cost is $15 per copy which you can pay by money order, credit card or check made out to NYC Department of Health. Include a self addressed, stamped envelop. It can take 4 to 8 weeks to get the copy. If you want a 2-3 day delivery, there is an additional fee of $11 for shipping and handling.

NEW YORK STATE (EXCLUDING NEW YORK CITY)
New York Vital Records
P.O. Box 2602
Albany, NY   12220-2602
Telephone: (518) 474-3077

Make your $15 check or money order payable to the New York State Department of Health. You will save time if you first call and ask what information they require. You can also request a certified copy from the registrar or town clerk of the city, town or village where the death occurred.

RECORDING THE DEATH CERTIFICATE

In New York, the New York State Department of Health issues the death certificate. The Department does not publish the death certificate so it is not part of the public record. If the decedent owned real property in New York, then it is important to record the decedent's death certificate in each county in which the decedent owned property. If the deed to real property is in the name of a husband and his wife, then once the death certificate is recorded any one who examines the county record will know that the surviving spouse now owns the property. Nothing more need be done to establish that ownership. If, however, the decedent owned the property in his name only, then some sort of probate procedure will be necessary so that a new deed can be recorded to establish the identity of the new owner.

In New York, the Clerk in the county where the property is located, will record a certified copy of the death certificate. Some counties have a Register instead of a Clerk to record deeds. Chautauqua and Cattaraugus, require that deeds be recorded in each township within those counties (Real Property 291). You may need to submit several copies of the death certificate for recording in those counties. Call the county clerk and ask where to mail the death certificate and how much money you need to send for the recording fee. Enclose a self addressed, stamped, envelop for the Clerk to return the recorded death certificate so you will have a record of where each death certificate was recorded.

If the decedent owned property in another state, then a death certificate should be recorded in the county where that property is located. You will need to call the clerk in each county for information about how to record the death certificate in that county.

About Probate

Once a person dies, all of the property he owns as of the date of his death is referred to as the *decedent's estate.* If the decedent owned property that was in his name only (not jointly or in trust for someone), then some sort of court procedure is necessary to determine who is entitled to possession of the property. The name of the court procedure is *probate.*

The root of the word probate is "to prove." It refers to the first job of the probate court, that is, to examine proof of whether the decedent left a valid Will, i.e. he died *testate* or whether he died *intestate* (without a valid Will). The second job of the probate court is to appoint someone to wrap up the affairs of the decedent — to pay any outstanding bills and then to distribute what property is left to the beneficiaries.

If the decedent named someone in his Will to be the *Executor* of his estate, then the court will appoint that person for the job. If he died intestate, then the court will appoint someone to be the *Administrator* of the decedent's estate. In either case, the person appointed by the court to settle the decedent's estate is referred to as the decedent's *Personal Representative* (Estates 1-2.13).

There are different ways to conduct a probate procedure depending on the value of the probate estate and whether the decedent owned real property at the time of his death. The method of conducting a probate procedure is called the *estate administration.* Chapter 6 explains how to determine whether a probate procedure is necessary and if so, then what kind of administration is necessary.

Giving Notice Of The Death 2

Those closest to the decedent usually notify family members and close friends by telephone. The funeral director will arrange to have an obituary published in as many different newspapers as the family requests, but there is still the job of notifying the government and people who were doing business with the decedent. That task belongs to the person named as Executor in the decedent's Will. If the decedent died without a Will, then New York statute (Surrogate's 1001) gives an order of priority for appointing someone to be appointed as the Personal Representative of the estate:

1st	surviving spouse
2nd	the decedent's children
3rd	the grandchildren
4th	the father or mother
5th	the brothers or sisters
6th	anyone entitled to the largest share of the decedent's estate

If no probate procedure is necessary, the job of notifying people of the death and settling the decedent's affairs falls to his spouse; and in the absence of a spouse, to the decedent's next of kin. By *next of kin,* we mean those people who inherit the decedent's property according to the New York Law of Intestate Succession. That law is explained in Chapter 5: NEW YORK'S INTESTATE LAW.

The person who has the job of settling the decedent's estate should begin to give notice as soon as is practicable after the death. Two government agencies that need to be notified are the Social Security Administration and the IRS. This chapter gives the telephone number of those as well as all the other agencies that need to be notified.

NOTIFYING SOCIAL SECURITY

Many Funeral Directors will, as part of their service package, notify the Social Security Administration of the death. You may wish to check to see that this has been done. You can do so by calling 1-800-772-1213. If you are hearing impaired call 1-800-325-0778 TTY. You will need to give the Social Security Administration the full legal name of the decedent as well as his social security number and date of birth.

> *Special Situation* >>> FOR DECEDENT RECEIVING SOCIAL SECURITY CHECKS

If the decedent was receiving checks from Social Security, then you need to determine whether his last check needs to be returned to the Social Security Administration.

Each Social Security check is a payment for the prior month, provided that person lives for the entire prior month. If someone dies on the last day of the month, then you should not cash the check for that month. For example, if someone dies on July 31st, then you need to return the check that the agency mails out in August. If however, the decedent died on August 1st then the check sent in August need not be returned because that check is payment for the month of July.

If the Social Security check is electronically deposited into a bank account, then notify the bank that the account holder died and notify the Social Security Administration as well. If the check needs to be returned, then the Social Security Administration will withdraw it electronically from the bank account. You will need to keep the account open until the funds are withdrawn.

SPOUSE ▶ THE SPOUSE AND CHILD'S SOCIAL SECURITY BENEFITS

If the decedent had sufficient work credits, the Social Security Administration will give the decedent's widow(er) or if unmarried, then the decedent's minor children, a one-time death benefit in the amount of $255.

SURVIVORS BENEFITS:

The spouse (or ex-spouse) of the decedent may be eligible for Survivors Benefits. Benefits vary depending on the amount of work credits earned by the decedent; whether the decedent had minor or disabled children; the spouse's age; how long they were married; etc.

The minor child of the decedent may be eligible for dependent child's benefits regardless of whether the decedent father ever married the child's mother. Paternity can be established by any one of several methods including the father acknowledging his child in writing or verbally to members of his family.

SOCIAL SECURITY BENEFITS

A spouse or ex-spouse can collect social security benefits based on the decedent's work record. This value may be greater than the spouse now receives. It is important to make an appointment with your local Social Security office and determine whether you as the spouse (or ex-spouse), or parent of the decedent's minor child, are eligible for Social Security or Survivor benefits. The SOCIAL SECURITY ADMINISTRATION has a web site from which you can down load publications that explain social security and survivor benefits.

SOCIAL SECURITY WEB SITE
http://www.ssa.gov

DECEDENT WITH
GOVERNMENT PENSION

If the decedent was a federal retiree and received a government pension, then any check received after the date of death needs to be returned to the U.S. Treasury. If the check is direct-deposited to a bank account, then call the financial institution and ask them to return the check. If the check is sent by mail, then you need to return it to: Director, Regional Finance Center
U. S. Treasury Department
P.O. Box 7367
Chicago, IL 60680

Include a letter explaining the reason for the return of the check and stating the decedent's date of death.

$$$ APPLY FOR BENEFITS $$$

Even though you notify the government of the death, they will not automatically give you benefits to which you may be entitled. You need to apply for those benefits by notifying the Office of Personnel Management ("OPM") of the death and requesting that they send you an application for survivor benefits. You can call 1-888-767-6738 or you can write to:
THE OFFICE OF PERSONNEL MANAGEMENT SERVICE
AND RECORDS CENTER
BOYERS, PA 16017

You will find brochures and information about Survivor's Benefits at the OPM web site:

Office of Personnel Management Web Site
http://www.opm.gov
You can get assistance via E-mail at
retire@opm.gov

In most cases, pension and annuity checks are payment for the prior month. If the decedent received his pension or annuity check before his death, then no monies need be returned. Pension checks and/or annuity checks received after the date of death may need to be returned to the company. You need to notify the company of the death to determine the status of the last check sent to the decedent.

Before notifying the company, locate the policy or pension statement that is the basis of the income. That document should tell whether there is a beneficiary of the pension or annuity funds now that the pensioner or annuitant is dead. If you cannot locate the document, use the return address on the check envelope and ask the company to send you a copy of the plan. Also request that they forward to you any claim form that may be required in order for the survivor or beneficiary to receive benefits under that pension plan or policy.

If the pension/annuity check is direct-deposited to the decedent's account, then ask the bank to assist you in locating the company and notifying the company of the death.

DECEDENT WITH AN
INDIVIDUAL RETIREMENT ACCOUNT ("IRA")
or a QUALIFIED RETIREMENT PLAN ("QRP")

Anyone who is a beneficiary of an IRA or QRP needs to keep in mind that no income taxes have been paid on monies placed in an IRA or QRP account. Once monies are withdrawn, significant taxes may be due. You need to learn what options are available to you as a beneficiary of the plan and the tax consequences of each option. You will need to ask an accountant or tax attorney how much will be due in taxes for each option. Once you know all the facts, you will be able to make the best choice for your circumstance.

SPOUSE If the spouse is the beneficiary of the decedent's IRA account, then there are special options available. The spouse has the right to withdraw the money from the account or roll it over into the spouse's own retirement account. Although the employer can explain options that are available, the spouse still needs to understand the tax consequence of choosing any given option. It is important to consult with an accountant or tax attorney to determine the best way to go.

If the decedent had a QRP, the plan may permit the spouse to roll the balance of the account into a new IRA. The spouse needs to contact the decedent's employer for an explanation of the plan and all the options that are available at this time.

NOTIFYING IRS

THE FINAL INCOME TAX RETURN
The Personal Representative, or next of kin, needs to file the decedent's final state and federal income tax returns. This can be done as part of the income tax return for the year of his death. If you have a joint bank account with the decedent, do not close that account until you determine whether the decedent is entitled to an income tax refund. See Chapter 6 for an explanation of how to obtain a refund from the IRS and from New York State.

THE GOOD NEWS
Monies inherited from the decedent are generally not counted as income to you, so you do not pay federal income tax on those monies. If the monies you inherit later earn interest or income for you, then of course you will report that income as you do any other type of income.

Real and personal property inherited by a beneficiary is inherited at a "stepped up" basis. This means that if the decedent purchased some item that is now worth more than when he purchased it, then the beneficiary inherits the property at its fair market value as of the decedent's date of death. For example, suppose the decedent bought stock for $20,000 and it is now worth $50,000, then the beneficiary inherits the stock at the $50,000 value. If the beneficiary sells the stock for $50,000, he pays no capital gains tax. If the beneficiary holds onto the stock and later sells it or $60,000, the beneficiary will pay federal and New York State capital gains tax only on the $10,000 increase in value since the decedent's death.

WHEN TO EVALUATE THE PROPERTY

The IRS gives you a choice of taking the value of the decedent's estate as of his date of death or 6 months later. For example, suppose the decedent's estate consists of stock worth $100,000 and you decide to hold onto them. If they increase in value so that 6 months later they are worth 110,000, you can (by filing the proper IRS tax return) elect to evaluate the decedent's estate at the six-month value in place of the date-of-death value. If you sell the stock at that time, then you will not pay capital gains on the stock.

CAUTION If you hold onto the stock, there is a risk that it will decrease in value during that six month period. If the stock goes down to $80,000, and you then sell, your only consolation will be that you can reflect the loss on your income tax statement.

Also, you need to consider the cost of employing an accountant (or a tax attorney) to file the necessary forms for the 6-month election. If you hold onto the stock and the increase in value is only a few thousand dollars, it may not pay to take the election. The cost in time and expense to make the election could be more than the tax payment itself.

SPOUSE ➤ SELLING THE HOME

In the tough "ole days" the IRS used to allow a once-in-a-lifetime, over age 55, up to $125,000 capital gains tax exclusion on the sale of the homestead (the principal residence). If a married couple sold their home and took the exclusion it was "used up" and no longer available to the other partner. In these, the good times, the IRS allows you to sell your homestead and up to $250,000 ($500,000 for a married couple) of the home-sale profit is tax free (IRC Section 121 B 3). There is no limit on the number of times you can use the exemption, provided you own and live in the homestead at least 2 years prior to the sale.

If the decedent and his spouse used their "once in a lifetime" homestead tax exemption, with this new law, the surviving spouse can sell the homestead and once again take advantage of a tax break.

An *estate tax* is a tax imposed by New York State and the federal government for the transfer of property at death. The *taxable estate* of the decedent is the total value of all of his property, as of his date of death. This includes real property (homestead, condominiums, vacant lots, etc.) and personal property (cars, life insurance policies, business interests, securities, IRA accounts, etc.). It includes property held in the decedent's name alone, as well as property that   he held jointly or in trust for another.

The Federal government gives each person an Estate and Gift Tax Exclusion amount. No gift tax need be paid unless the decedent's taxable estate, plus gifts that he gave during his lifetime exceeding $10,000/per person per year, exceed the Exclusion amount. The Exclusion amount is scheduled to increase each year until the year 2006:

YEAR	TAXABLE ESTATE
2000 — 2001	$675,000
2002 — 2003	$700,000
2004	$850,000
2005	$950,000
2006	$1,000,000

No Federal or New York Estate tax return need be filed unless the decedent's taxable estate and lifetime gifts exceed the scheduled amount as of his date of death. If it does, then you need to employ an accountant or tax attorney to prepare an IRS Estate tax return (IRS form 706) and a New York Estate tax return (ET 90-706). There is an unlimited marital tax deduction, so if the decedent was married, no estate tax need be paid; however if the decedent's estate exceeds the stated value, a 706 must be filed.

Special Situation ▷ DECEDENT WITH A TRUST

If the decedent was the Grantor (or Settlor) of a trust, then he was probably managing the trust, as Trustee, during his lifetime. The trust document should name someone as **Successor Trustee** now that the Grantor is deceased. The trust document may instruct the Successor Trustee to make certain gifts once the Grantor dies, or perhaps hold money in trust for a beneficiary of the trust.

IF YOU ARE SUCCESSOR TRUSTEE

If you are the Successor Trustee, then in addition to following the terms of the trust, you are required to obey all of the laws of the state of New York relating to the administration of a trust. For example, you are required to keep all trust property separate from your own individual property (Estates 11-1.6). You are required to give an accounting to anyone who has an interest in the trust — that includes the beneficiaries of the trust as well as the decedent's creditors (Surrogate's 2210). You should consult with an attorney experienced in Trust and Estate matters to explain how to properly administer the trust and to ensure that you do so without any liability to yourself.

IF YOU ARE A BENEFICIARY

If you are a beneficiary of the trust, then you need to obtain a copy of the trust and see how the trust is to be administered now that the Grantor or Settlor is deceased. Most trust documents are written in "legalese," so you may want to employ your own attorney to review the trust, and explain what rights you have under that trust.

People and companies who were doing business with the decedent need to be notified of his death. This includes utility companies, credit card companies, banks, brokerage firms and any company that insured the decedent.

NOTIFY CREDIT CARD COMPANIES

You need to notify the decedent's credit card companies of the death. If you can find the contract with the credit card company check to see whether the decedent had credit card insurance. If the decedent had credit card insurance, then the balance of the account is now paid in full. If you cannot find the contract contact the company and get a copy of the contract along with a statement of the balance due as of the date of death.

DESTROY DECEDENT'S CREDIT CARDS

You should destroy all of the decedent's credit cards. If you hold a credit card jointly with the decedent, then it is important to waste no time in closing that account and opening another in your name only. Consider the case of John and Barbara. They never married but they did live together for several years before he died from AIDS. John came from a well to do family so he had enough money to support himself and Barbara during his illness. John put Barbara on all of his credit card accounts so that she could purchase things when he became too ill to go shopping with her. After the funeral, Barbara had a gathering of friends and family at their apartment. Barbara was so preoccupied with her loss that she never noticed that John's credit cards were missing.

Barbara did not know who ran up the bills on John's credit cards during the month following his death. It was obvious that John's signature had been forged — but who forged it? One credit card company suspected that it might have been Barbara herself. Because the cards were held jointly, Barbara became liable to either pay the debts or prove that she did not make the purchases. She was able to clear her credit record but it took several months and she had to employ an attorney to do so.

NOTIFY INSURANCE COMPANIES

Examine the decedent's financial records to determine the name and telephone number of all of the companies that insured the decedent or his property. This includes real property insurance, motor vehicle insurance, health insurance and life insurance.

LIFE INSURANCE COMPANIES

If the decedent had life insurance, then you need to locate the policy and notify the company of his death. Call each life insurance company and ask what they require in order to forward the insurance proceeds to the beneficiary. Most companies will ask you to send them the original policy and a certified copy of the death certificate.

Send the original policy by certified mail or any of the overnight services that require a signed receipt for the package. Make a copy of the original policy for your records before mailing the original policy to the company.

IF YOU CANNOT LOCATE THE POLICY

If you know that the decedent was insured but you cannot locate the insurance policy, the AMERICAN COUNCIL OF LIFE INSURANCE ("ACLI") may be able to help you. Write to the ACLI giving them the name, address, date of birth, and social security number of the decedent.   Their address is:

POLICY SEARCH ACLI
1000 Pennsylvania Avenue, NW
Washington, DC 20004

The ACLI will assist you by asking the 100 largest insurance companies in the nation to search their records for the missing policy.   If it is found, you will receive a copy of the policy free of charge.

IF YOU CANNOT LOCATE THE COMPANY

If you cannot locate the insurance company it may be doing business under another name or it may no longer be doing business in the state of New York. Insurance companies are highly regulated. Each state has a branch of government that regulates insurance companies. If you are having difficulty locating the insurance company call the Department of Insurance in the state where the policy was purchased and ask for assistance in locating the company.   The number for the New York Department of Insurance is (800) 342-3736. For the hearing impaired call (800)220-9250.

 THE EAGLE PUBLISHING COMPANY OF BOCA web site gives the telephone number of the Department of Insurance for each state: http://www.eaglepublishing.com

HOMEOWNER'S INSURANCE

If the decedent owned his own home, then check whether there is sufficient insurance coverage on the property. The decedent may have neglected to increase his insurance as the property appreciated in value. If you think the property may be vacant for some period of time, then consider having vandalism coverage included in the policy.

Once the property is sold, or transferred to the proper beneficiary, you can have the policy discontinued or transferred to the new owner. The decedent's estate should receive a rebate for the unused portion of the premium.

NOTIFYING THE HOMEOWNER'S ASSOCIATION

If the decedent owned a condominium or a residence regulated by a homeowner's association, then the association needs to be notified of the death. Once the property is transferred to the proper beneficiary, he/she will need to contact the association and arrange to have notices of dues or assessments forwarded to the new owner.

MORTGAGE INSURANCE

If the decedent had a mortgage on any parcel of real estate that he owned, he might have arranged with his lender for an insurance policy that pays off the mortgage balance in the event of his death. Look at the closing state-ment to see if there was a charge for mortgage insurance. Also, check with the lender to determine if such a policy was purchased.

If the decedent was the sole owner of the property, then the beneficiary of that property needs to make arrangements to continue payment of the mortgage until title to the property is transferred to that beneficiary.

MOTOR VEHICLE INSURANCE

If the decedent owned any type of motor vehicle (car, truck, boat, airplane) locate the insurance policy on that vehicle and notify the insurance company of the death. Determine how long insurance coverage continues after the death. Ask the insurance agent to explain what things are covered under the policy. Is the motor vehicle covered for all types of casualty (theft, accident, vandalism, etc.) or is coverage limited in some way?

If you can continue coverage then determine when the next insurance payment is due. Hopefully, the car will be sold or transferred to a beneficiary before that date, but if not, then you need to arrange to continue with insurance coverage.

 *Special Situation* **ACCIDENT INSURANCE**

If the decedent died as a result of an accident, then check for all possible sources of accident insurance coverage including his homeowner's policy. Some credit card companies provide free accident insurance as part of their contract with their card holders. If the decedent died in an automobile accident, then check to see whether he was covered by any type of travel insurance, such as rental car insurance. If he belonged to an automobile club, such as AAA, then check whether he had insurance as part of his club membership.

```
┌─────────────────┐
│ Special         ╲
│ Situation        ╲    BUSINESS OWNED BY DECEDENT
└──────────────────╱
```

If the decedent owned his own company he may
have purchased "key man" insurance. Key man
insurance is a life insurance policy designed to protect
the company should a valuable employee die.
Benefits are paid to the company to compensate the
company for the loss of someone who is essential to
the continuation of the business. Ultimately the policy
benefits those who inherit the business.

If the decedent owned shares in the company or was
a partner in the company, there may be a shareholder's
agreement or partnership agreement that requires
the company to use the insurance proceeds to
purchase the shares or buy out the partnership
interest owned by the decedent. If there is a probate
procedure, then the Personal Representative's attorney
will need to review the agreement. If the decedent
died without a Will, then the next of kin needs to
investigate the matter to determine what rights (if any)
the family has in the business or to the proceeds of an
insurance policy.

Special Situation	DECEDENT OWNER OR REGISTERED AGENT OF A CORPORATION

If the decedent was the sole owner and officer of a corporation, then the New York Division of Corporations needs to be notified of the change. There may need to be a probate procedure to determine the new owner of the company so it may take some period of time before new officers and directors are identified.

If the decedent was the registered agent of a corporation, then a new agent needs to be appointed and a Certificate of Change filed with the Division of Corporations. A Certificate of Change form can be obtained by calling the Division at (518) 473-2492. There is a $30 charge to file the Certificate of Change.

STATUS REPORT

If you were not actively involved in running the business, then you might request a status report of the company. The report will show whether filing fees are current and will identify the officers and directors of the company. You can obtain a status report by calling (900) 835-2677 or by writing to:

> Department of State
> Division of Corporations, State Records
> 41 State Street
> Albany, NY 12231-0001

HEALTH INSURANCE

If the decedent had health insurance, the insurance carrier probably knows of the death, but it is a good idea to contact them to determine what coverage the decedent had under that insurance plan. If you cannot find the original policy, have the insurance company send you a copy of the policy so that you can determine whether medical treatment given to the decedent before his death was covered by that policy.

DECEDENT ON MEDICARE

If the decedent was covered by Medicare, you do not need to notify anyone, but you do need to know what things were covered by Medicare so that you can determine what medical bills are (or are not) covered by Medicare. The publication MEDICARE AND YOU explains what things are covered. You can get it the publication by writing to:

U.S. GOVERNMENT PRINTING OFFICE
U.S. Dept. of Health and Human Services
Health Care Financing Administration
7500 Security Boulevard
Baltimore, MD 21244-1850

You can also find the publication at the HEALTH CARE FINANCING ADMINISTRATION ("HCFA") Web Site:

HCFA WEB SITE
http:/www.medicare.gov

If the spouse of the decedent is insured under Medicare, then the death does not affect the surviving spouse's coverage.

If you have questions about Medicare coverage, there is a toll-free Medicare Hotline (800)633-4227. English and Spanish speaking operators are available Monday through Friday from 8 a.m. to 4:30 p.m. For the hearing impaired call TTY/TDD (877) 486-2048.

HEALTH INSURANCE COVERAGE FOR THE SPOUSE

SPOUSE ▷

If the spouse was covered under the decedent's health insurance policy then he/she needs to arrange for new coverage. If the decedent was employed by a federally regulated company (a company with at least twenty employees), then under the Consolidated Omnibus Budget Reconciliation Act ("COBRA") the employer must make the company health plan available to the surviving spouse and any dependent child of the decedent for at least 36 months. The employer must notify the spouse and/or dependent child of their right to continue insurance coverage. They have 60 days from the date of death or 60 days after notice is sent by the employer (whichever is later) to notify the employer whether they wish to continue under the plan.

The only problem with continued coverage may be the cost. Before the death, the employer may have been paying some percentage of the premium. The employer has no such duty after the death unless there was some employment contract that states otherwise. Under COBRA, the employer may charge the spouse for the full cost of the plan plus a 2% administrative fee. You can find additional information about COBRA in the publication **PENSION AND HEALTH CARE COVERAGE** as well as other information about the U.S. Department of Labor publications at their Web site:

DEPARTMENT OF LABOR WEB SITE
http://www.dol.gov/dol/pwba

The state of New York has a continued health care coverage law similar to the federal statute (Insurance 3221 (m)). Between federal and state statute, the spouse should be able to continue health care coverage after the decedent's death.

✍ CHANGE BENEFICIARY ✍

If the decedent was someone you named as beneficiary of your insurance policy, Will or trust, brokerage account or pension plan, then you may need to name another beneficiary in his place:

INSURANCE POLICY ✍

If you named the decedent as the primary beneficiary of your life insurance policy, then check to see whether you named a contingent (alternate) beneficiary in the event that the decedent did not survive you. If not, then you need to contact the insurance company and name a new beneficiary. If you did name a contingent beneficiary, then that person is now your primary beneficiary and you need to consider whether you wish to name a new contingent beneficiary at this time.

HEALTH INSURANCE POLICY ✍

If the decedent was covered under your health insurance policy, then your employer and the health insurer need to be notified of the death because this may affect the cost of the plan to you and/or your employer.

WILL OR TRUST ✍

Most Wills provide for a contingent beneficiary in the event that the person named as beneficiary dies first. If you named the decedent as your beneficiary, then check to see whether you named an alternate beneficiary. If not, you need to have your attorney revise your Will and name a new beneficiary.

Similarly, if you are the Grantor or Settlor of a trust and the decedent was one of the beneficiaries of your trust, then check the trust document to see if you named an alternate beneficiary. If not, contact your attorney to prepare an amendment to the trust, naming a new beneficiary.

BANK/SECURITIES ACCOUNT ✍

If the decedent was a beneficiary of your bank or securities account, or if the decedent was a joint owner of your bank account or securities account, then it is important to contact the financial institution and inform them of the death. You may wish to arrange for a new beneficiary or joint owner at this time.

PENSION PLANS ✍

If the decedent was a beneficiary under your pension plan, then you need to notify them of his death and name a new beneficiary. Many pension plans require that you notify them within a set period of time (usually 30 days) so it is important to notify them as soon as you are able.

If the decedent was a beneficiary of your Individual Retirement Account ("IRA") or of your Qualified Retirement Plan ("QRP") and you did not provide for an alternate beneficiary, then you need to name someone at this time.

There are many government regulations relating to IRA and QRP accounts. For example, you must begin to withdraw money from the account on April 1st of the year after you reach the age of 70 1/2. How much you must withdraw depends on a number of things including whether you choose to base the amount withdrawn on your own life expectancy or on the joint life expectancy of you and your oldest beneficiary.

If you have not reached the age of 70 1/2, then before naming a new beneficiary, you may wish to consult with your accountant or estate planning attorney to decide which is the best option for you.

NOTIFYING CREDITORS

If the decedent owed money, and a probate procedure is necessary, then it will be the job of the person who is appointed as Personal Representative to give written notice of the death to all of the decedent's creditors. The attorney who handles the probate will explain to the Personal Representative how notice is to be given.

If no probate procedure is necessary, then the next of kin can notify the creditors of the death, but before doing so, first read Chapter 4: WHAT BILLS NEED TO BE PAID? Chapter 4 explains what bills need to be paid and who is responsible to pay them, but before any bill can be paid, you need to know what the decedent owned as of his date of death. The next chapter explains how to identify, and then locate all of the property owned by the decedent.

Locating the Assets 3

It is important to locate the financial records of the decedent and then carefully examine those records. Even the partner of a long-term marriage should conduct a thorough search because the surviving spouse may be unaware of all that was owned (or owed) by the decedent.

It is not unusual for a surviving spouse to be surprised when learning of the decedent's business transactions — especially in those cases where the decedent had control of family finances. One such example is that of Sam and Henrietta. They married just as soon as Sam was discharged from the army after World War II. During their marriage, Sam handled all of the finances, giving Henrietta just enough money to run the household.

Every now and again Henrietta would think of getting a job. She longed to have her own source of income and some economic independence. Each time she brought up the subject Sam would loudly object. He had no patience for this new "woman's lib" thing. Sam said he got married to have a real wife — one who would cook his meals and keep house for him.

Henrietta was not the arguing type. She rationalized, saying that Sam had a delicate stomach and dust allergies. He needed her to prepare his special meals and keep an immaculate house for him. Besides, Sam had a good job with a major cruise line and he needed her to accompany him on his frequent business trips.

Once Sam retired, he was even more cautious in his spending habits. Henrietta seldom complained. She assumed the reason for his "thrift" was that they had little money and had to live on his pension.

They were married for 52 years when Sam died at the age of 83. Henrietta was 81 at the time of his death. She was one very happy, very angry and very aged widow when she discovered that Sam left her with assets worth well over a million dollars!

LOCATING FINANCIAL RECORDS

To locate the decedent's assets you need to find evidence of what he owned and where those assets are located. His financial records should lead you to the location of all of his assets so your first job is to locate those records. The best place to start the search is in the decedent's home. Many people keep their financial records in a single place but it is important to check the entire house to be sure you did not miss something.

CHECK THE COMPUTER
Don't overlook that computer sitting silently in the corner. It may hold the decedent's check register and all of the decedent's financial records. The computer may be programmed to protect information. If you cannot access the decedent's records, you may need to employ a computer technician or computer consultant who will be able to print out all of the information on the hard drive of the computer. You can find such a technician or consultant by looking in the telephone book under
COMPUTER SUPPORT SERVICES   or
COMPUTER SYSTEM DESIGNERS & CONSULTANTS.

COLLECT AND IDENTIFY KEYS

The decedent may have kept his records in a safe deposit box, so you may find that your first job is to locate the keys to the box. As you go through the personal effects of the decedent, collect and identify all the keys that you find. If you come across an unidentified key, it could be a key to a post office box (private or federal) or a safe deposit box located in a bank or in a private vault company. You will need to determine whether that key opens a box that contains property belonging to the decedent or whether the key is to a box no longer in use. Some ways to investigate are as follows:

☑ CHECK BUSINESS RECORDS

If the decedent kept receipts, look through those items to see if he paid for the rental of a post office or safe deposit box. Also, check his check register to see if he wrote out a check to the Postmaster or to any safe deposit or vault company. Look at his bank statements to see if there is any bank charge for a safe deposit box. Some banks bill separately for safe deposit boxes so check with all of the banks in which the decedent had an account to determine if he had a box with that bank.

☑ CHECK THE KEY TYPE

If you cannot identify the key take the key to all of the local locksmiths and ask whether anyone can identify the type of facility that uses such keys. If that doesn't work then go to each bank, post office and private safe deposit boxes located in places where the decedent shopped, worked or frequented and ask whether they use the type of key that you found.

☑ CHECK THE MAIL

Check the mail over the next several months to see if the decedent receives a statement requesting payment for the next year's rental of a post office or safe deposit box.

You may find evidence of a brokerage account, bank account, or safe deposit box by examining correspondence addressed to the decedent. If the decedent was living alone, then have the mail forwarded to the person he named as Executor or Personal Representative of his Will. If the decedent did not leave a Will, then the mail should be forwarded to his next of kin. Call the Postmaster and ask him/her to send you the necessary forms to make the change. Request that the mail be forwarded for the longest period allowed by law (currently one year).

The decedent may have been renting a post office box at his local post office branch or perhaps at the branch closest to where he did his banking. Ask the Postmaster to help you determine whether the decedent was renting a post office box. If so, then you need to locate the key to the box so that you can collect the decedent's mail.

 Special Situation > **LOST POST OFFICE BOX KEY**

If the decedent had a post office box and you cannot locate the key, then contact the local postmaster and ask him/her what documentation is needed for you to gain possession of the mail in that box. As before, you will ask the Postmaster to have all future mail addressed to that box, forwarded to the Personal Representative, or if there is no Will, then to the decedent's next of kin.

WHAT TO DO WITH CHECKS

You may receive checks in the mail made out to the decedent. Social security checks, pension checks and annuity checks issued after the date of death need to be returned to the sender (see pages 28 and 30 of this book). Other checks need to be deposited to the decedent's bank account. The decedent is not here to endorse the check, but you can deposit to his account by writing his bank account number on the back of the check and printing beneath it "FOR DEPOSIT ONLY." The bank will accept such an endorsement and deposit the check into the decedent's account. If the check is significant in value and/or the decedent had different accounts that are accessible to different people, then there needs to be cooperation and a sense of fair play. If not, the dollar gain may not nearly offset the emotional turmoil. Such was the case with Gail.

Gail's father made her a joint owner of his checking account to assist in paying his bills. He had macular degeneration and it was increasingly difficult for him to see. The father also had a savings account that was in his name only.

Gail's brother, Richard, had a good paying job in California. Even though he lived at a distance, Richard, his wife and two children would always spend the spring school break holidays with his father. Gail's good cooking added to the festivities. Winters were still another time for a visit with Richard and his family. Their father enjoyed leaving the cold northeastern climate to spend a few weeks in the warm California sunshine. Just before Christmas, the father purchased a round trip ticket to California. It cost several hundred dollars. Before the departure date, the father had a heart attack and died.

Gail called the airline to cancel the ticket. They refunded the money with a check made out to her father. She deposited the check into the joint account.

As part of the probate procedure, the money in the father's savings account was divided equally between Richard and his sister. Richard wondered what happened to the money from the airline tickets. Gail explained "He paid for the tickets from the joint account, so I deposited the money back to the joint account. "
"Well aren't you going to give me half?"
"Dad meant for me to have whatever was in that joint account. If he wanted you to have half of the money, he would have made you joint owner as well."

Richard didn't see it that way:
"That refund was part of Dad's probate estate. It should have been deposited to his savings account to be divided equally between us. Are you going force me to argue this in court?"

Gail finally agreed to split the money with Richard, but the damage was done.

Gail complains that holidays are lonely since her father died.

LOCATE OUT OF STATE ACCOUNTS
If the decedent had out of state bank or brokerage accounts, then you might be able to locate them if they mail the decedent monthly or quarterly statements. Not all institutions do so, but all institutions are required to send out an IRS tax form 1099 each year giving the amount of interest earned on that account. Once those forms come in, you will learn the location of all of the decedent's active accounts.

COLLECT LEGAL DOCUMENTS

As you go through the papers of the decedent you may come across documents that indicate property ownership, such as bank registers, title to motor vehicles, stock or bond certificates, insurance policies, brokerage account statements, etc. Place all evidence of ownership in a single place. You will need to contact different institutions to transfer title to the proper beneficiary. Chapter 5 explains how to identify the proper beneficiary. Chapter 6 explains how to transfer the property to that beneficiary. See Chapter 6 if you cannot find the title to a motor vehicle.

COLLECT DEEDS

Collect the deeds to all property owned by the decedent. Many people keep deeds in a safe deposit box. If you cannot find the deed in the decedent's home, then you need to determine whether he had a safe deposit box. If you know that the decedent owned real property (lot, residence, condominium, cooperative, time share, etc.) but you cannot locate the deed, then contact the Clerk's office, in the county in which the property is located, and ask for a copy of the deed.

You will need to identify the parcel of land by giving the legal description of the land or its parcel identification number. You can find this information on the last tax bill sent to the decedent. If you cannot find the last tax bill, then call the County Assessor's office and they will give you the information.

You can use the same procedure if you cannot locate the deed to property owned by the decedent in another state, namely, check with the recording department in the county where the property is located. Some states keep their land records in the court house. If such is the case, then check with the Clerk of the County or Circuit Court.

LOCATE CONTRACTS

If the decedent belonged to a health club or gym, he may have prepaid for the year. Look for the club contract. It will give the terms of the agreement. If you cannot locate the contract then contact the company for a copy of the agreement. If the contract was prepaid, then determine whether the agreement provides for a refund for the unused portion.

SERVICE CONTRACT

Many people purchase appliance service contracts to have their appliances serviced in the event that an appliance should need repair. If the decedent had a security system then he may have a service contract with a company to monitor the system and contact the police in the event of a break-in. If the decedent had a service contract, then you need to locate it and determine whether it can be assigned to the new owner of the property. If the contract is assignable, the new owner can reimburse the decedent's estate for the unused portion. If the contract cannot be assigned, then once the property is transferred, try to obtain a refund for the unused portion of the contract.

 **LAWYER**

DECEDENT OWNER OF ONGOING BUSINESS

If the decedent had his own business or was a partner or shareholder of a small company, then the Personal Representative (or next of kin, if he died intestate) needs to contact the company accountant to obtain the company's business records. If there is a company attorney, then contact the attorney for assistance in continuing to operate the business or terminating it. If you are a beneficiary of the estate, consider consulting with your own attorney to determine your rights and responsibilities in the business.

RESIDENTIAL LEASE

If the decedent was renting his residence, then he may have a lease agreement. It is important to locate the lease because the decedent's estate may be responsible for payments under the lease. If you cannot find a lease, then ask the landlord for a copy. If the landlord reports that there was no lease, then verify with the landlord that the decedent was on a month to month basis. You will need to work out a schedule to vacate the premises.

If a written lease is in effect, then determine the end of the lease period. If that date is more than a couple of months away, then ask the landlord whether he will agree to cancel the lease on the condition that the property is vacated in good condition.

If the landlord is not willing to cancel the lease, then the landlord has the right to make a claim on the decedent's estate for monies owed. If no one starts a probate procedure, then after 3 months from the date of death, the landlord can sue the surviving spouse for monies the decedent owed under the lease. If there is no surviving spouse, then he can sue the lineal descendants; and if no lineal descendants, then anyone who is entitled to inherit the decedent's property (Real Property 711 (2)).

If the landlord wants to hold the estate liable for the balance of the lease, then it is prudent to have an attorney review the lease to determine what rights and responsibilities remain now that the tenant is deceased.

COLLECT TAX RECORDS

You will need to file the decedent's final state and federal income tax return so you need to collect all of his tax records for the past 3 years. If you cannot locate his prior tax records, then check his personal telephone book and/or his personal bank register to see if he employed an accountant. If you can locate his accountant, then contact the accountant to see if he/she has a copy of those records.

If you are unable to locate the decedent's federal tax records, then they can be obtained from the IRS. The IRS will send copies of the decedent's tax filings to anyone who has a *fiduciary relationship* with the decedent. The IRS considers the following people to be fiduciaries:

➤ the person named as Personal Representative of the decedent's Will

➤ the successor trustee of the decedent's trust

➤ if the person died intestate, then whoever is legally entitled to possession of the decedent's property (See Chapter 5 to learn who are the beneficiaries.)

To notify the IRS of the fiduciary capacity, you need to file Form 56: NOTICE CONCERNING FIDUCIARY RELATIONSHIP
To request the copies, file IRS Form 4506:
    REQUEST FOR COPY OR TRANSCRIPT OF TAX FORM
Your accountant can file these forms for you or you can obtain the forms from the IRS by calling (800) 829-3676 or you can download them from the Internet:

IRS FORMS WEB SITE
http://www.irs.gov./forms_pubs/forms.html

NEW YORK STATE INCOME TAX RETURN

If you cannot locate the decedent's state income tax return you can get copies from the New York State Income Tax department by calling (800) 225-5829 or you can write to: New York State Income Tax
Centralized Photocopy Unit
W.A. Harriman Campus, Bldg.8
Albany, NY 12227

They charge 25 cents per page. As with the IRS, the state will require some proof of a fiduciary relationship from the person making the request. They will also request the decedent's social security number and the last address that he used to file his return.

You can obtain information about New York State taxes from the New York State Income Tax Web Site. The web site contains tax forms that you can download.

 NEW YORK STATE INCOME TAX
WEB SITE
http://www.tax.state.ny.us/

FINDING LOST/ ABANDONED PROPERTY

If the decedent was forgetful, he might have lost or abandoned property, such as a bank account, contents of a safe deposit box, a stock or brokerage account, travelers checks, pay checks, money orders, annuities, or insurance funds, etc. The person or institution who has possession of unclaimed property must try to locate the owner of the property. If they are unsuccessful, then they must turn over the property to the New York State Comptroller. There are different time periods in which property is identified as being unclaimed. For example, if an employee does not claim his wages, then after 1 year, the wages are declared as unclaimed and then turned over to the state. For bank accounts it is 5 years; for traveler's checks or money orders, it is 15 years (Abandoned Property 300, 303, 1308, 1309).

The State Comptroller puts all unclaimed funds into an Abandoned Property Fund. The Personal Representative or the decedent's next of kin can check to see if there is any unclaimed property belonging to the decedent by calling (518) 474-4038 or by writing to:

> State Comptroller, Office of Unclaimed Funds
> Alfred E. Smith Building, 9th Floor
> Albany, NY 12236

The State Comptroller has a Web Site that you can use to check whether the decedent has any unclaimed funds in the state of New York:

 NEW YORK STATE COMPTROLLER WEB SITE
http://www.osc.state.ny.us/

CLAIMS FOR DECEDENT VICTIMS OF HOLOCAUST

The New York State Banking Department has a special Claims Processing Office for Holocaust survivors or their heirs. The office processes claims for Swiss bank accounts that were dormant since the end of World War II. You can call them for information at (800) 695-3318.

CLAIMS IN OTHER STATES

Each state has an agency or department that is responsible for handling lost, abandoned or unclaimed property located within that state. If the decedent had residences in other states, then call the UNCLAIMED or ABANDONED PROPERTY department to see if the decedent has unclaimed property in that state.

EAGLE PUBLISHING COMPANY OF BOCA
lists telephone numbers for the
unclaimed property division for
each state at their web site:
www.eaglepublishing.com

LOCATING THE WILL

If you have possession of the original Will, you need to deposit it with the Clerk of the Surrogate's Court in the county in which the decedent lived.   There is only one original Will, so it is important to hand carry the original document to the Registrar. If you are unable to make the delivery in person, you can mail the Will to the Registrar, but send it by certified mail so that you will have proof of delivery. Make a copy of the Will for your own records before delivering it to the court.

You may wish to call the clerk for directions to the Surrogate's court, and also to learn of the best time to meet with the clerk to avoid a wait in line.

If you do not have the Will but believe someone has it in their possession, or perhaps may have even destroyed the Will, then you have the right to ask the Surrogate's Court to require that person to come before the court and be questioned about the matter (Surrogate's 1401). You will need to employ an attorney who is experienced in Probate matters to file the petition asking the court to compel that person to either produce the Will or give testimony about the location of the Will.

Special Situation   WILL DRAFTED IN ANOTHER STATE OR COUNTRY

The state of New York respects the laws of other states. If a Will is drafted in another state and the Will is valid in that state, then it is valid here (Estates 3-5.1). If the Will has not been witnessed or notarized, then the court may require witnesses to swear that the Will is valid and has not been revoked (Surrogate's 1404, 1405, 1406).

If the Will was drafted in another country and is written in a foreign language, then it will need to be accompanied by a true and complete English translation before it can be admitted to Probate.

If you have any Will that is not drafted in conformity with New York law, you will need to employ an attorney, who is experienced in probate matters, to get a Will admitted to probate. We will discuss what makes a Will valid in the state of New York in chapter 5.

☎ LAWYER   A COPY AND NO ORIGINAL

If you have a copy of the Will but cannot locate the original, then New York law allows the estate of the decedent to be probated using the copy, provided you can prove that the document is a true copy of the decedent's valid, unrevoked Will (Surrogate's 1407). You will need to employ an attorney who is experienced in probate matters to present such proof to the court.

DECEDENT WITH
OUT OF STATE RESIDENCE

If the decedent had his principal residence in another state, then before you deposit the Will with the Surrogate's Court, consult with an attorney experienced in Probate matters to determine whether the Will needs to be probated in New York or in the state where the decedent lived. If the Will is to be probated in another state, then it is best to contact an attorney in that state and arrange to have the original Will deposited with the Probate court in the state where the decedent had his principal residence.

DECEDENT WITH
OUT OF STATE PROPERTY

If the decedent owned property in New York and in another state, you may need to have a probate procedure in New York and an *ancillary* (secondary) probate procedure in the other state. It could be done the other way around; that is, you could have the probate in the other state and the ancillary procedure in New York.

The Personal Representative (or next of kin, if no Will) should consult with an attorney in each state to determine the best course of action. Convenience and cost are important considerations, but you also need to consider that each state has its own tax structure and probate statutes. Ask each attorney whether the location of the probate procedure will have any effect on who is to inherit the property or how much the estate will be taxed.

THE MISSING WILL

It is estimated that 70% of the population do not have a Will, so if you cannot find a Will, chances are that the decedent did not have one. If you think that the decedent had a Will, but you cannot find it, then try to locate the decedent's check book for the past few years and see whether he paid any attorney fees. If you are able to locate the decedent's attorney, then call and inquire whether the attorney ever drafted a Will for the decedent, and if so, whether the attorney has the original Will in his possession.

If the attorney has the original Will, then ask the attorney to forward the Will to the Surrogate's court. Asking the attorney to forward the Will to the court does not obligate you to employ the attorney should you later find that a formal probate procedure is necessary.

If you believe that the decedent had a Will but you cannot find it, then check to see if the decedent had a safe deposit box. If he did, you will need to gain entry to that box to see whether the Will is in the box. See the next page for an explanation of how to gain entry to the safe deposit box.

ACCESSING THE SAFE DEPOSIT BOX

Once you notify a bank in New York that the lessee of a safe deposit boxes is dead, they will seal the box and not allow anyone access to that box until a court orders the bank to turn over the contents of the box to someone — usually the Personal Representative of the decedent's estate.

If someone was joint lessee with the decedent or if the decedent gave someone (his "deputy") authority to access his safe deposit box, then the bank will allow that person to examine the contents of the safe deposit box under the supervision of a bank officer. The bank officer will allow the joint lessee or deputy to make a copy of any document that gives instructions for the decedent's funeral or burial. This could be a deed to a cemetery plot, or perhaps proof of membership in a burial society. The bank will not allow anything else to be removed from the box without a court order (Surrogate's 2003 (2)).

If the decedent was the only one with authority to access his safe deposit box, then the bank will not allow anyone to even look at the contents of the box without an order from the judge of the Surrogate court. If, after reading Chapter 6 of this book, you find that you will need to go through probate, then you can get that order as part of the probate procedure. But what if you find that you can get possession of the decedent's property without going through probate. Do you need to start a probate procedure just to be able to look in his safe deposit box?

You do not need to start a probate procedure, but you will still need to get a court order. New York statute (Surrogate's 2003) allows a person to petition (ask) the judge of the Surrogate Court for an order authorizing that person to do the following:

⇨   examine the contents of the box in the presence
         of an officer of the bank
⇨   make an inventory of the contents of the box
⇨   remove the deed to the burial plot
⇨   delivery an insurance policy to the beneficiary
         named in the policy
⇨   deliver the Will to the clerk of the Surrogate's Court.
(Surrogate's Court 2003).

Notice the statute does not allow anything other than the Will, deed to plot and insurance policy to be removed from the box, so it may turn out that you will still need to have a probate procedure to get anything else that you may find in the safe deposit box. See Chapter 6 HOW TO GET SAFE DEPOSIT BOX CONTENTS for information about how to get the order and the contents of the box.

What Bills Need To Be Paid? 4

New York is a state that respects the rights of creditors. If the Probate estate of the decedent has sufficient assets, then the Personal Representative has the duty to be sure that all of the decedent's valid bills are paid. If the decedent had many debts, there may not be sufficient funds to pay all of the bills. The only remaining question is whether anyone else is responsible to pay those bills. If the decedent was married, then the first person the creditor will look to, is the decedent's spouse.

The reason creditors seek payment from the spouse are based in history. Under English Common law, a husband was legally held responsible for his wife's debts. The English believed it reasonable for the husband to assume this duty because once a woman married, her legal identity merged with that of her husband. A married woman had no right to own property or to enter into a contract in her own name. She became totally dependent on her husband and he was legally responsible to provide her with basic necessities — food, clothing, shelter and medical services. If anyone provided these necessities to his wife, then, regardless of whether the husband agreed to be responsible for the debt, he became obliged to pay for them. This law was called the DOCTRINE OF NECESSARIES.

The United States inherited its legal system from England, but over the years each state developed its own set of laws relating to spousal responsibility. Some states decided to make the Doctrine of Necessaries part of their state law. Other states, such as New Jersey, decided to apply the Doctrine equally to both sexes, making the husband responsible to pay for his wife's necessaries and the wife responsible to pay for her husband's necessaries. Other states abolished the law altogether. For example, in Florida, courts have ruled that the creditor cannot collect from the spouse unless the spouse agreed to pay the debt.

In New York, the Doctrine was not made part of the state law, however New York courts have ruled that if a creditor cannot collect payment for necessaries from the debtor, then the creditor can require payment from his or her spouse. (*Our Lady of Lourdes Memorial Hospital, Inc. v. Frey.*, 152 A.D.2d 73, 548 N.Y.S.2d 109 (1989).

In this chapter we will discuss who is responsible to pay debts left by the decedent, beginning with joint debts.

JOINT DEBTS

A *joint debt* is a debt that two or more people are responsible to pay. Usually the contract or promissory note reads that both parties agree to *joint and severable* liability, meaning they both agree to pay the debt and each of them, individually, agree to be pay the debt. A joint debt can also be in the form of monies owed by one person with payment guaranteed by another person. If the person who owes the money does not pay, then the *guarantor* is responsible to pay the debt.

Before paying a bill, determine whether it is the decedent's debt or a joint debt. Hospital bills, nursing home bills, funeral expenses, legal fees incurred because of the decedent's death are all debts of the decedent's estate. They are not joint debts unless someone guaranteed payment for the monies owed.

PAYING FOR THE JOINT DEBT

If another person is jointly responsible for monies owed by the decedent, then that bill should be paid from any joint account held with the decedent. If the joint debtor did not have a joint account with the decedent, then the joint debtor must pay the bill from his/her own funds.

SPOUSE ⟶ JOINT DEBTS WITH SPOUSE

Loans signed by the decedent and his spouse are joint debts, as are charges on credit cards that both were authorized to use. Property taxes are a joint debt if the decedent and the spouse both owned the property.

JOINT PROPERTY BUT NO JOINT DEBT

Suppose all of the decedent's funds are held jointly with a family member and the joint owner of the account did not agree to pay those debts?   Can the creditor require that half of the joint funds be set aside to pay the debt?

The answer to this question depends on how the joint property is titled.   As we will see in Chapter 5 there are different ways to hold property jointly with another.   If two people hold property jointly *with rights of survivorship*, then the surviving owner owns the property as of the date of death. If the property is held by two people as a *tenancy-in-common*, then each owns half. The surviving owner has no right of survivorship. The decedent's creditors have the right to demand that the decedent's share of the account be used to pay his debt.

Under New York law, unless the bank account states otherwise, it is presumed that a deposit account (including CD's) in two or more names, is tenancy-in-common (Estates 6-2.2(a)). This means that if the New York bank account does not specifically state that the surviving owner has rights of survivorship, then as soon as the bank is notified of the death, they will freeze the account, until an Personal Representative is appointed and takes possession of the decedent's share of the account.

NO MONEY — NO PROPERTY

If the decedent owed money, then the bill needs to be paid from assets owned by the decedent — which leads to the next question "Did the decedent have any money in his own name when he died?"

If the decedent died without any money or property in his name, then there is no money to pay any creditor. The only question that remains is whether anyone else is liable to pay those bills. As we discussed, if the decedent is married, and the bill was for necessaries, then the spouse must pay the bill regardless of whether the spouse signed any contract agreeing to make such payment.

But what if the decedent was single, can anyone else be made liable? The issue of payment most often arises in relation to services provided by nursing homes. When a person enters a nursing home, he is usually too ill to speak for himself or even sign his name. In such cases, the nursing home administrator will ask a family member to sign a battery of papers on behalf of the patient before allowing the patient to enter the facility. Buried in that battery of papers may be a statement that the family member agrees to be responsible for payment to the nursing home. If the family member refuses to guarantee payment and the patient's finances are limited, then the facility may refuse to admit the patient.

If a nursing home accepts Medicare or Medicaid payments, then under the Federal Nursing Home Reform Law, that nursing home is prohibited from requiring a family member to guarantee payment as a condition of allowing the patient to enter that facility. USC Title 42 §1395I-3(c)(5)(A)(ii). Nonetheless, it is common practice for nursing home, in effect, to say "Either someone agrees to pay for the patient's bill or you need to find a different facility."

Since most nursing homes are business establishments and not charitable organizations, the nursing home must be paid for the services they provide or they soon will be out of business. For an insolvent patient, the solution to the problem is to have the patient admitted to a facility as a Medicaid patient.

But what if the decedent had some money when he entered the nursing home and you agreed to guarantee payment to the nursing home?

What if you feel that you were coerced into signing as a guarantor?

Are you now liable to pay the decedent's final nursing home bill if your family member died without funds?

An experienced Elder Law attorney will be able to answer these questions after examining the documents that you signed and the conditions under which the patient entered the nursing home.

AN ESTATE WITH ASSETS

If the decedent owed money and he died owning property, belonging to him alone, such as a bank account, securities, or real property, then there may be money available to pay monies owed by the decedent. It is up to the decedent's Personal Representative to pay all valid debts, but to do so the Personal Representative first must gain possession of the decedent's assets. To gain possession of the decedent's assets, there will need to be some sort of probate procedure to determine who is entitled to the decedent's property.

Once the probate procedure begins, all of the decedent's creditors will be given an opportunity to come forward and produce evidence showing how much is owed. The Personal Representative needs to look over each unpaid invoice and decide whether it is a valid bill. The problem with making that decision is that the decedent is not here to say whether he actually received the goods and services now being billed to his estate.

This is especially the case for medical or nursing care bills. An example of improper billing brought to the attention of this author was that of a bill submitted for a physical examination of the decedent. The bill listed the date of the examination as July 10th, but the decedent died on July 9th. Other incorrect billings may not be as obvious, so each invoice needs to be carefully examined.

If the Personal Representative decides to challenge a bill, and is unable to settle the matter with the creditor, then the Probate court will decide whether the debt is valid and should be paid.

MEDICAL BILLS COVERED BY INSURANCE

If the decedent had health insurance you may receive an invoice stamped "THIS IS NOT A BILL." This means the health care provider has submitted the bill to the decedent's health insurance company and expects to be paid by them. Even though payment is not requested, it is important that you verify that the bill is valid for two reasons:

➢ LATER LIABILITY

If the insurer refuses to pay the claim, the facility will seek payment from whoever is in possession of the decedent's property, and that may reduce the amount inherited by the beneficiaries.

➢ INCREASED HEALTH CARE COSTS

Regardless of whether the decedent was covered by a private health care insurer or Medicare, improper billing increases the cost of health insurance to all of us. Consumers pay high premiums for health coverage. We, as taxpayers, all share the cost of Medicare. If unnecessary or fraudulent billing is not checked, then ultimately, we all pay.

 *Special Situation* **MEDICARE FRAUD**

If you believe that you have come across a case of Medicare fraud, you can call the ANTI-FRAUD HOTLINE 1-800-447-8477 and report the incident to the Office of the Inspector General of the United States Department of Health and Human Services.

HOW TO CHECK MEDICARE BILLING

If the decedent was covered by Medicare, then an important billing question is whether the health care provider agreed to accept Medicare *assignment of benefits*, meaning that they agreed to accept payment directly from Medicare. If so, the maximum liability for the patient is **20%** of the amount determined as reasonable by Medicare. For example, suppose a doctor bills Medicare $1,000 for medical treatment of the decedent. If Medicare determines that a reasonable fee is $800, then the patient is liable for 20% of the $800 ($160).

Health care providers who do not accept Medicare assignment bill the patient directly. They can charge up to 15% more than the amount allowed by Medicare. If the decedent knew and agreed to be liable for the payment, then his estate may be liable for whatever Medicare doesn't pay. For example, if a doctor's bill is $1,000 and Medicare allows $800, then Medicare will reimburse the decedent's estate 80% of $800 ($640). The doctor may charge the estate 15% more than the $800 ($920) and the estate may be liable for the difference: $920 - $640 or $280.

To summarize:
For health care providers accepting Medicare assignment, the most they can bill the decedent's estate is 20% of what Medicare pays (not 20% of what they bill.)

Those who do not accept Medicare assignment, can bill 15% more than the amount allowed by Medicare. The decedent's estate may be liable for the difference between the amount billed and the amount paid by Medicare.

In either case, if the decedent had secondary health care insurance, then the secondary insurer may be responsible to pay the difference. If you have a question about Medicare billing call:
 MEDICARE PART B CUSTOMER SERVICE 1-800-333-7586.

| Special Situation | DENIAL OF MEDICARE COVERAGE |

If the health care provider reports to you that services provided to the decedent are not covered by Medicare, or if the facility submits the bill to Medicare and Medicare refuses to pay, then check to see if you agree with that ruling by determining what services are covered under Medicare. See page 45 of this book for information about how to obtain pamphlets that explain what medical treatments are covered under Medicare.

If you believe that the decedent has wrongly been denied coverage, then you can appeal that decision. The MEDICARE RIGHTS CENTER is a private nonprofit organization partially funded by the New York State Office For The Aging. They will assist you with your Medicare appeal. Their service is free of charge. You can reach them at 1-800-333-4144.

If you wish to have an attorney assist with your Medicare appeal, then you can call your local Bar Association for a referral to an attorney experienced in Medicare appeals. Some attorneys work *pro bono* (literally for the public good; i.e. without charge) but most charge to assist in an appeal. Federal statute 42 U.S.C. §406(a)(2)(A) limits the amount an attorney may charge for a successful medical appeal to 25% of the amount recovered or $4,000, whichever is the smaller amount.

SOMETHINGS ARE CREDITOR PROOF

Sometimes it happens that the decedent had money or property titled in his name only, but he also had a significant amount of debt. In such cases the beneficiaries may wonder whether they should go through a probate procedure if there will be little, if anything, left after the creditors are paid. Before making the decision consider that some assets are protected under New York law:

✧ THE HOMESTEAD ✧

New York property owned and occupied by a person as his/her main residence is called *homestead* property. The **equity** in the homestead is the current value of the property less monies owed on the property. If there is less than $10,000 equity in the property, then no creditor can force the sale of the property. There are exceptions to this rule. Creditor protection does not extend to delinquent taxes or mortgages on the homestead (Civil Practice 5206).

If the decedent was married, then the homestead exemption continues for his spouse and minor child — but only until the spouse dies and his children have all reached the age of 18. If the decedent was single then the homestead exemption is lost and a creditor can ask the Probate court to have the homestead sold in order to pay the decedent's debts.

✧ EXEMPTIONS FOR BENEFIT OF FAMILY ✧

If the decedent had his principal residence in New York and he was married at the time of his death, then upon his death the surviving spouse owns the following items:

(1)　all household furniture, appliances, computers, musical instruments and furnishings used in and about the house, up to $10,000 in value;

(2)　the family bible, family pictures, video tapes, computer discs, software and books, not exceeding $1,000 in value;

(3)　domestic animals and necessary food for 60 days, farm machinery, one tractor and one lawn tractor, not exceeding $15,000 in value;

(4)　one motor vehicle not exceeding $15,000 in value. The spouse can elect to take cash instead of the decedent's motor vehicle (up to $15,000). If the decedent owned more than one vehicle, then the spouse has his/her choice of motor vehicle. If the vehicle chosen is worth more than $15,000 the spouse must pay the difference to the estate. If the decedent's made a gift of the vehicle in his Will, then the spouse can still chose that vehicle, and the value of the car will be paid to the intended beneficiary.

(5)　money or other personal property not exceeding $15,000 in value, except if there is not enough money to pay for the funeral. In that case the funeral is paid and the balance of the $15,000 belongs to the spouse.

The *value* of each of these items is its *net value*, i.e., its fair market value, less any monies owed on that item. If the items described in (1) to (4) are not in existence, then no substitutions of money or property can be made.

These 5 items are called EXEMPT PROPERTY because in a probate procedure the spouse may ask the probate court to exempt these items from the claims of creditor — except for monies owed on the item. For example, if money is owed on the car, then the spouse needs to pay off the loan, otherwise the lender is entitled to repossess the car.

If there is no surviving spouse, but the decedent left children under the age of 21, then they are entitled to share these exemptions between them. If the decedent was single, with no children under the age of 21, then none of these items are exempt from the claims of creditors (Estates 5-3.1).

✧ FEDERAL RETIREMENT PLANS ✧

Federal retirement plans 401, 402(a)5, 403 (a) (4), 408 A or 408 (d)(3) (IRA and Keogh accounts) are exempt from the claims of creditors. All monies received by beneficiaries of these plans are protected from the decedent's creditors (Civil Practice 5205 (c) (2)).

✧ INSURANCE AND ANNUITIES ✧

If a life insurance policy or an annuity policy is payable to a beneficiary, then these monies are not available to pay debts owed by the decedent (Civil Practice 5205 (c) (2)).

✧ THERE IS A PRIORITY OF PAYMENT ✧

Not all probate debts are equal. New York statute (Surrogate's 1811) establishes an order of priority for payment of claims made against the decedent's estate:

CLASS 1:   COST OF ADMINISTRATION
Top priority goes to the cost of the probate procedure including attorney's fees and fees charged by the Personal Representative.

CLASS 2:   FUNERAL EXPENSES
Second in priority are the decedent's reasonable funeral expenses. This includes the cost of the funeral, a church or other service, the burial lot, a suitable monument and perpetual care of the burial site (Surrogate's 103 (22)).

CLASS 3:   TAXES
Any debt that has preference under federal or state law. This includes estate and income taxes and other monies owed by the decedent to the state or federal government.

CLASS 4:   PROPERTY TAXES
If the decedent owned real property and taxes were assessed on that property prior to his death, then the Personal Representative must pay that tax.   Whoever inherits that property must reimburse the Personal Representative unless the decedent's Will requires the taxes be paid from the Probate estate.

CLASS 5:   JUDGMENTS
Judgments against the decedent are paid in chronological order, i.e., the judgment with the earliest date is the first to be paid. If any money is left, then the judgment with the next earliest date is paid, etc.

CLASS 6:   ALL OTHER DEBTS
If any money is left after all the prior classes are paid, then the Personal Representative will use it to pay all of the decedent's valid debts.

Except for Class 5, there is no order of priority for any other class of debt. All the debtors in a given class have the same right to be paid. If there is not enough money to pay all of the creditors in a given class, then the Personal Representative will prorate the available funds.

If the monies owed on a Class 6 debt are secured by collateral, for example a loan on a car or a mortgage on real property, then the Personal Representative can ask the court to allow the collateral to be given to the creditor as partial or complete satisfaction of the debt.

If there is any dispute about the payment of a debt, the Probate court will decide who is to be paid and how much they will receive.

Special Situation

DECEDENT ON MEDICAID

Medicaid is a program that provides medical and long term nursing care for people with low income and limited resources. The program is funded jointly by the federal and state government. Federal law 42 U.S.C. 1396(p) requires the state to put into effect a plan to recover monies spent from the estate of a deceased Medicaid recipient. Usually there are no monies to recover because to qualify for Medicaid in New York, a person may have no more than $3,600 in non-exempt assets.

Sometimes it happens that a person on Medicaid dies and his estate later receives money perhaps as part of a cash settlement of a lawsuit. The state has the right to be reimbursed for government funds spent on the decedent during his lifetime. In such case, the state of New York becomes a preferred creditor of the decedent's estate.

✧ THERE IS A STATUTE OF LIMITATIONS ✧

Finally, consider that there is a statute of limitations for bringing a claim against the Probate Estate of the decedent. The Personal Representative must inform the decedent's creditors that the decedent died, and that a probate procedure is in progress. If the Personal Representative knows the identity of a creditor, then he must give the creditor notice by mail. If a creditors does not file his claim within 7 months after the date of the appointment of the Personal Representative, then his claim is essentially barred (Surrogate's 1802).

But what if no one starts a probate procedure?
If the decedent owed money, and no one starts a Probate procedure, then after 18 months, the creditor can start an action in any civil court that hears such cases. If the creditor is successful, he can force whoever is heir to that property to either pay the debt or sell the property and use the proceeds from the sale to satisfy that debt.

If the decedent was sued prior to his death and has a judgment that was placed against his real property, then that lien continues for two years after the decedent's death, or 10 years after the filing of the judgment-roll, which ever is later (Civil Practice 5208). During that time, the creditor can start a civil court procedure to force the heir to that property to either pay the debt or sell the property and use the proceeds to pay the judgment.

Bottom line, if the decedent had property in his name only, then even if you do not start a Probate procedure, a creditor can go to court and ask the court to order that the decedent's property be sold to pay the debt.

MONIES OWED TO THE DECEDENT

Suppose you owed money to the decedent? Do you need to pay that debt now that he is dead? That depends on whether there is some written document that says the debt is forgiven once the decedent dies. For example, suppose the decedent lent you money to buy your home. If he left a Will saying that once he dies, your debt is forgiven, then you do not need to make any more payments. If you signed a mortgage at the time and if that mortgage was recorded, then the Personal Representative of the decedent's estate should sign and record a satisfaction of that mortgage. If you signed a promissory note then the Personal Representative should mark the promissory note "PAID IN FULL" and return the original note to you.

If you owed the decedent money and there is no Will, or if there is a Will, no mention of forgiving the debt, then you still owe the money. If you borrowed the money from the decedent and his spouse, then you need to pay the debt to the spouse. If you borrowed the money from the decedent only, then the debt becomes an asset to the estate of the decedent, meaning that you now owe the money to the decedent's heirs. If you are one of those heirs, you can deduct the money from your inheritance.

For example, suppose your father left $70,000 in a bank account to be divided equally between you and your two brothers. If you owed your father $20,000, then your father's estate is really worth $90,000. Instead of paying the $20,000, you can agree to receive $10,000 and have the $20,000 debt forgiven. Each of your brothers will then receive $30,000 in cash.

Who Are The Beneficiaries? 5

A question that comes up early on is who is entitled to the property of the decedent. To answer the question you first need to know how the property was titled (owned) as of the date of death.

There are three ways to own property. The decedent could have owned property jointly with another person; or in trust for another person; or the decedent could have owned property that was titled in his name only.

In general, upon the decedent's death:

Joint Property belongs to the surviving joint owner.

Trust Property belongs to the beneficiary of the trust.

Property owned by the **decedent only** belongs to beneficiaries named in the Will.
If there is no Will, then the property goes to his heirs as per the New York Laws of Intestate Succession.

NOTE ⇨ If the decedent was married, then his spouse may have rights in his property.

This chapter explains each of these types of ownership in detail.

PROPERTY HELD JOINTLY

Bank accounts, securities, motor vehicles, real property can all be owned jointly by two or more people. If one of the joint owners dies, then the survivor(s) continue to own their share of the property. Who owns the share belonging to the decedent depends on how the joint ownership was set up.

THE JOINT BANK ACCOUNT

If the decedent and another person are joint owners on an account — each with the ability to withdraw funds on his own signature, then the surviving owner of that account is free to withdraw all of the funds and close it out (Banking 675).

If a joint bank account is held in three names, each with authority to make withdrawals, then when one of the joint owners dies any one of the remaining owners can withdraw all of the funds in the account. With such an arrangement, the remaining owners need to cooperate with each other to divide the account equitably.

JOINTLY HELD SECURITIES

You can determine whether the decedent owns a security (stock, bond) alone or jointly with another by examining the face of the stock or bond certificate. If two names are printed on the certificate followed by a statement that the security is held jointly, then the surviving owner can either cash in the security or ask the company to issue a new certificate in the name of the surviving owner. You will need to forward a certified copy of the death certificate to the company and ask that they send you the necessary forms to make the change.

If the decedent held securities in a brokerage account, then the name of the owner of that account is printed on the monthly or quarterly brokerage statement. Not all brokerage houses print the name of a joint owner on the brokerage statement so you need to contact the brokerage house and request a copy of the contract that is the basis of the account. It may be that the account is held jointly, or perhaps the decedent named a beneficiary who now inherits the account. The contract will show the terms of the brokerage account. If you determine that the account is held jointly or for the benefit of someone, then have the brokerage firm forward the necessary forms to make the transfer to the proper owner or beneficiary.

THE CONVENIENCE ACCOUNT

If the decedent needed assistance with his finances, he may have added someone to his bank or securities account for his own convenience and not with the intent of giving that person any right to the monies in the account. If that is the case, then the name on the account should reflect that intent, for example:

ALFRED RAY and ENID RAY, for the convenience of ALFRED RAY

This is not a joint account. Should Alfred die, then Enid has no right to this account. The account becomes part of Alfred's estate. The account is the same as if it were held in Alfred's name only (Banking 678)

THE JOINTLY HELD MOTOR VEHICLE

If a motor vehicle is held jointly, the name of each owner is printed on the title to the motor vehicle. In New York, if two names are on the title, either person has the right to transfer the car on his own signature. If one person dies, the other owns the car, 100%. You can change title to the car to your name only when the registration and/or car insurance expires.

It may be prudent to change title prior to that time. You might be able to get a reduced insurance rate if there is only one person insured under the policy. Also, should you be involved in an accident, by changing title officially, then there is no question but that you are the sole owner and the estate of the decedent is in no way liable for the accident.

REAL PROPERTY HELD JOINTLY

The name of the owner of real property is printed on the face of the deed. To determine whether the decedent owned the property jointly with another person, you need to look at the last recorded deed. (See page 57 if you cannot locate the deed.)

The top paragraph of the deed identifies the person who transferred the property (the "Grantor") and the person who is now the owner of the property (the "Grantee"). For example:

"This indenture, made this day, March 15, 1999, between
ROBERT TRAYNOR, party of the first part
hereinafter referred to as the Grantor, and

JOSE CAVALLO and RICHARD CAVALLO as JOINT TENANTS,
party of the second part,
hereinafter referred to as the Grantee ....."

Once you have possession of the last recorded deed look at the person who is named as the "GRANTEE" or the "PARTY OF THE SECOND PART." Whoever is so identified, is the owner of the property as of the decedent's date of death.

If the deed identifies two or more persons as "joint tenants" (as in the above example) and one of the joint tenants dies, then the surviving tenant owns the property.

THE SURVIVING JOINT OWNER

Once a joint owner dies, the survivor owns the property and is free to take possession of the property or sell it. The surviving owner does not need to do anything to establish his ownership, but the decedent's name is still on the deed. As explained in Chapter 1, when the death certificate is recorded, then the fact that the decedent is dead becomes part of the public record.

If the surviving owner later sells the property, the buyer will learn from the public record that the joint owner is dead, but the buyer will still want to be assured that there are no taxes that might be a lien on the property as a result of the decedent's death. The closing could be delayed while the closing agent scrambles to obtain a tax release from the New York Department of Revenue.

If you are the surviving joint owner you can avoid this problem by having your accountant or attorney apply for a release from the Department of Revenue. When it is received you can have the release recorded along with the death certificate. Once these documents are recorded, you can sell the property without any delay caused by the decedent's death.

Even if you don't intend to sell the property, it is important that you take care of these matters soon after the decedent's death. If you don't, then whoever inherits the property from you will need to get two tax releases, one for you and one for the decedent. That could be difficult to do if many years have passed since the decedent's death, and his tax records have been lost or destroyed.

▤ DEED HELD AS TENANTS IN COMMON

If the Grantee of a deed identifies the decedent and another as TENANTS IN COMMON, then the decedent's share belongs to whomever the decedent named as his beneficiary in his Will. If the decedent died without a Will, then the New York Laws of Intestate Succession determine who inherits the property. See page 100 for an explanation of the law.

If a deed names two or more people as Grantee, but does not say whether they are Joint Tenants or Tenants In Common, then according to New York statute they hold title as Tenants in Common (Estates 6-2.2).

If property is owned by the decedent as a Tenant In Common, then a probate procedure is necessary. Once it is determined who has the right to inherit the property, the attorney for the Personal Representative will prepare a new deed that identifies the new owners of the property.

🗐 DEED HELD AS HUSBAND AND WIFE

If the Grantee on the deed is identified as a married couple, for example: TODD AMES AND SUSAN AMES, H/W
or
TODD AMES AND SUSAN AMES, HIS WIFE
or
TODD AMES AND SUSAN AMES, HUSBAND AND WIFE
or
TODD AMES AND SUSAN AMES, TENANTS BY ENTIRETY
then when one spouse dies, and providing they are still married at the time of death, the surviving spouse owns the property 100% even though the deed still shows the two names (Estates 6-2.2 (c)).

The surviving spouse should have the death certificate recorded to establish that there is now one owner. As explained on the previous page, it is a good idea to have your accountant or attorney obtain and record a release from the Department of Revenue at the same time.

 DIVORCED PRIOR TO DEATH

If the decedent was divorced prior to his death, then even though the deed says that the couple holds the property as husband and wife, they don't. The divorce decree should state who now owns the property. It could be that the decedent owns the property, or his ex-spouse may own it, or they could each own half as Tenants-In-Common. If you cannot find a deed that was recorded after the divorce, then you need to consult with an attorney experienced in Estate or Real Property matters to determine who now owns the property.

▤ DEED WITH A LIFE ESTATE

A **Life Estate** interest in real property means that the person who owns the Life Estate has the right to live in that property until he/she dies. While the owner of the Life Estate is alive, the Grantee has no right to occupy the property. Once the owner of the Life Estate dies, the property belongs to the person who is named as Grantee on the deed.

You can identify a Life Estate interest by examining the face of the deed. If somewhere on the face of the deed you see the phrase RESERVING A LIFE ESTATE to the decedent, then the Grantee(s) can now occupy and take possession of the property. For example, suppose the granting paragraph of the deed reads:

THIS INDENTURE, made this day
between PETER REILLY
hereinafter referred to as "Grantor"

and, RACHEL SMITH
hereinafter referred to as "Grantee"

RESERVING A LIFE ESTATE TO THE GRANTOR

Once Peter dies, all Rachel need do is record the death certificate to establish her ownership of the property.

| Special Situation > | OUT OF STATE PROPERTY |

This chapter relates only to real property owned by the decedent in the state of New York. If the decedent owned property in another state or country, then the laws of that state or country determine who will inherit that property and you will need to consult with an attorney in that state to determine who owns the property now that the Grantee is dead.

 INVALID DEED

The discussion about who now owns real property left by the decedent presumes that you are in possession of the most recent valid deed. This may not be the case. The decedent could have signed a different deed after the deed you have in your possession.

Before you come to any conclusion about who inherits the property it is advisable to have an attorney, or a title company, do a title search to determine the owner of the property as of the decedent's date of death.

PROPERTY HELD IN TRUST

BANK/ SECURITY ACCOUNTS

If a bank account or securities brokerage account is held in the name of the decedent "in trust for" or "for the benefit of" someone, then once the bank has a certified copy of the death certificate, the bank will turn over the account to the beneficiary. Sometimes such accounts are referred to as a *Totten Trust Account.*

If the bank or security account is registered in the name of the decedent "as trustee under a trust agreement," that means the decedent was the trustee of a trust and the bank will turn over that account to the Successor Trustee of the trust. Banks usually require a copy of the trust when the account was opened, so the bank probably knows the identity of the Successor Trustee. If the trust was amended to name a different Successor Trustee, you need to present the bank with a copy of that amendment together with a certified copy of the death certificate.

MOTOR VEHICLE

If the motor vehicle is held in the name of the decedent "as trustee," then the motor vehicle is part of the trust property. The motor vehicle remains in the trust once the decedent trustee dies. The Successor Trustee will need to contact the motor vehicle bureau to have title changed to that of the Successor Trustee.

REAL PROPERTY HELD IN TRUST

If the decedent had a trust and put property that he owned in the trust, then the deed may read something like this:

THIS INDENTURE
made this day between
JOHN ZAMORA,
hereinafter referred to as "Grantor"

and JOHN ZAMORA, **trustee of the JOHN ZAMORA TRUST AGREEMENT**
DATED FEBRUARY 26, 1999
hereinafter referred to as "Grantee"

Once the trustee (John Zamora) dies, then that property remains in the trust. The trust document will say whether the person who takes John's place as trustee (the Successor Trustee) should sell or keep the property or perhaps give it to a beneficiary. If no instruction is given, then what the Successor Trustee does with the property may be affected by laws relating to the administration of trust property in the state where the property is located. If you are a beneficiary of the trust and you are concerned about what the Successor Trustee will do with the property, then it is best to consult with your attorney.

PROPERTY IN DECEDENT'S NAME ONLY

If the decedent owned property that was in his name only (not jointly or in trust for someone), then that property is identified as the decedent's *Probate Estate*. It is called the Probate Estate because some sort of probate procedure will be necessary before the heirs can get possession of that property. Who is entitled to the decedent's Probate Estate depends on whether the decedent died *testate* (with a Will) or *intestate* (without a Will):

If the decedent died testate, then the beneficiaries of the decedent's property are identified in the Will. If the decedent died intestate, then the state of New York provides a Will for him in the form of a set of intestate laws entitled: RULES GOVERNING INTESTATE SUCCESSION.

These laws determine who inherits the decedent's intestate probate estate and what percentage of the probate estate each heir is to receive once all the bills and costs of administering the probate are paid. The law recognizes the right of the family to inherit the decedent's property. The law covers all possible relationships beginning with the decedent's spouse.

NEW YORK'S INTESTATE LAW

✧ MARRIED, NO CHILDREN

The Rules Governing Intestate Succession provides that if at the time of death the decedent was married and had no surviving *lineal descendants* (children, grandchildren, great-grandchildren, etc.), then all of the probate estate goes to the surviving spouse (Estates 4-1.1 (a)(2)).

✧ NOT MARRIED, WITH CHILDREN

If the decedent was not married when he died, but had lineal descendants, then they inherit all of his property *by representation*. New York statute (Estates 1-2.16) defines the term "by representation" as follows:

> By representation means a disposition or distribution of property made in the following manner to persons who take as issue of a deceased ancestor:
>
> The property so passing is divided into as many equal shares as there are (i) surviving issue in the generation nearest to the deceased ancestor which contains one or more surviving issue and (ii) deceased issue in the same generation who left surviving issue, if any. Each surviving member in such nearest generation is allocated one share. The remaining shares, if any, are combined and then divided in the same manner among the surviving issue who are allocated a share had predeceased the decedent without issue.

If you understood the above definition and you are not a lawyer, then you missed your calling. For the rest of us (even lawyers) its a head-scratcher. Perhaps the best way to explain the term is by example.

ALL CHILDREN SURVIVE

Suppose the decedent was unmarried with 4 children, Ann, Barry, Carl, David and he dies intestate, then each of his children get 25% of his estate.

CHILD WITHOUT DESCENDANTS DIES BEFORE DECEDENT

If Ann dies before her father leaving no descendants, then Barry, Carl and David divide the estate between them and each gets one third.

CHILDREN WITH DESCENDANTS DIES BEFORE DECEDENT

Suppose instead that only Carl and David survived their father. If Ann died leaving 2 children and Barry died leaving 3 children, then the estate is divided into 4 shares — one for each surviving child and one share for each deceased child who left descendants. Carl and David each get their share, namely Carl gets 25% of the estate and David gets 25%. The remaining 50% gets divided equally among the 5 grandchildren, each getting 10% of the estate.

✧ MARRIED WITH CHILDREN

If the decedent was married, then his spouse is entitled to $50,000 plus half of whatever is left of the probate estate after all the bills and expenses are paid. The decedent's children get the other half, by representation (Estates 4-1.1 (a)(1)).

◈ SINGLE, NO CHILDREN

If the decedent had no children, then the property is divided equally between his parents, unless the parent failed or refused to provide for the child during his formative years (under the age of 21). If the parent later makes amends and establishes a parent-child relationship that continues to the child's death, then it may be that the parent can inherit the property (Estates 4-1.4). If there is any question about the parents legal (or moral) right to inherit, an attorney experienced in probate matters should be consulted.

If only one of the decedent's parents is alive, then all of the property goes to that parent. If neither parent is alive, then the estate goes to the decedent's brothers and sisters by representation. If the decedent had a relation by half blood, such as a half-brother, then he inherits the same as if he were of whole blood (Estates 4-1.1 (5) and (7b)).

If the decedent had no brothers, sisters, nephews or nieces, then the decedent's probate estate is divided in half with half going to the decedent's next of kin on his mother's side and the other half going to the decedent's next of kin on his father's side. New York statute (Estates 4-1.1 (6) and (7)) explains the order of distribution in detail. The order of distribution is fairly complex, so if a relation inherits at this level it is best to consult with an attorney before you decide who is entitled to the decedent's intestate property.

◈ THE STATE: HEIR OF LAST RESORT

If a person dies without a Will and he has absolutely no relations, then his property goes to the state of New York. The property is considered to be abandoned property and is regulated by the New York's abandoned property law (Estates 4-1.5).

If one joint owner is convicted of the first or second degree murder of another joint owner, then he is not entitled to inherit the joint owner's share of the bank account. If a trial is in progress, the court can freeze the bank account pending the outcome of the trial (Estates 4-1.6).

If anyone committed a wrongful act against the decedent that caused injury to the decedent or led to his death, then the Personal Representative can sue that person on behalf of the beneficiaries of the estate. If the Personal Representative refuses to sue, the beneficiaries can ask the court to appoint an administrator to prosecute on their behalf (Estates 5-4.1). Depending on the nature of the injury, the court may award punitive damages to the estate. The court will decide how the money is to be distributed. The court will award the greater amount to those who have suffered most from the loss. If the person who committed the act was a beneficiary of the estate, then of course that person gets none of the award and the share he would have received can be used to satisfy the judgment (Estates 5-4.3).

THE RIGHTS OF THE CHILD

ADOPTED CHILD
An adopted child has the same right to inherit as does a natural child of the decedent (Estates 1-2.10).

UNBORN CHILD
A child who is conceived during the decedent's lifetime, but born after the decedent dies, has the same right to inherit as one born during the decedent's lifetime (Estates 4-1.1 (c))

NON-MARITAL CHILD
A child born out of wedlock has the same rights to inherit from his/her natural father as does one born in wedlock, provided:

☑ the decedent acknowledged the child as his own by signing a legal document

— or —

☑ paternity was established by clear and convincing evidence and the decedent openly treated the child as his own (Estates 4-1.2).

 **LAWYER** | DECEDENT DENIED PATERNITY

If the decedent denied his paternity, then it will take a court procedure to establish (or disprove) paternity. If you want to establish paternity, then you will need to consult with an attorney who is experienced in litigation. If DNA tests need to be conducted, but the family plans to cremate the decedent, you may need to have your attorney move quickly to bar cremation until the matter is settled.

RIGHTS OF CHILD UNDER THE WILL

We discussed the rights of children when the parent dies without a Will, but suppose the decedent left a Will and did not include anything for a child. Is that child entitled to some part of the decedent's estate? The answer is "no," provided the decedent left a valid Will clearly stating that it was the decedent's wish not to give anything to the child. But suppose, the decedent made no mention of the child. Suppose, he simply "forgot" to include something for that child or perhaps he made the Will before the child was born. In such case, the child may have rights in that estate:

THE AFTERBORN CHILD

If the decedent had no children when he made his Will, then any child born after the date of the Will is entitled to as much of the decedent's estate as if he died intestate. If the decedent had one or more children and made a Will giving nothing to any of them and a child is born after the date of the Will, then that child gets nothing as well. But if the decedent left property to his children, then an afterborn child is entitled to his share of the gift given to his siblings. For example, suppose the decedent had two children and he gave them $75,000 each. If the decedent doesn't change his Will to include the third child, then that child is entitled to share in the $150,000 gift to the children. Each child will receive $50,000.

But suppose the Will made it clear that he intended to make the gift to the children who were alive at the time of the gift?

In that case, the afterborn child gets as much of the decedent's estate as if the decedent died without a Will. Whether the third child comes out better depends on the size of the estate. If the decedent had a large estate, the two children get to keep their $75,000 and the afterborn child may inherit far more than that amount. But, if the decedent was not married and all he had was the $150,000, then the result will be the same as before, namely each child gets $50,000 (Estates 5-3.2)

 THE "FORGOTTEN" CHILD

Suppose the decedent made a Will and neglected to make any mention of that child in his Will. The child could challenge the Will arguing that the decedent simply "forgot" to include something for that child. Such challenge will probably provoke a court battle. The named beneficiaries, will no doubt argue that the decedent was estranged from the "forgotten" child, and that the omission was deliberate.

If you wish to challenge a Will on this, or any other ground, you can expect a court battle. You will need to employ an attorney experienced in litigation matters to do so.

WHEN TO CHALLENGE THE WILL

If the decedent left a Will, then the Will states who is to receive the property — provided the Will is valid. In the state of New York for decedent's Will to be effective and enforceable, then at the time the decedent made the Will:

➤ he was 18 years of age or older

➤ he was of sound mind and memory, meaning he knew what he was doing (namely making a Will); what property he had, and who of his relatives would, under ordinary circumstances, expect to inherit his property

➤ he signed the Will in the presence of at least two witnesses (Estates 3-1.1 and 3-2.1).

If the decedent left a Will, then the Will states who is to receive the property. Most Wills are short and easy to read, however, you may come across an unfamiliar legal term such as the term *per stirpes*, for example:

"I leave the rest, residue and remainder of my
property to my children, Ann, Barry and Carl,
in equal shares, per stirpes."

This means that if a child dies before the decedent, then the share intended for that child is to be divided equally among the lineal descendants of that child (Estates 1-2.14).

Sometimes, a Will is ambiguous or can be read in two different ways. In such case, it is important to consult with an attorney, before deciding "who gets what.'

THE HOLOGRAPHIC WILL

The decedent may have left a Will that he wrote in his own hand, but no one witnessed him signing the Will. Such a Will is called a *holographic Will.* The state of New York does not recognize such a Will as being valid unless the Will was written by a member of the armed forces while he was in combat. Once the soldier returns from battle he must write one in conformity with New York law because the holographic Will is not accepted as valid if it has been more than a year since the soldier returned from battle.

Similarly, a mariner at sea may make a holographic Will, but that Will can only be accepted into probate if he dies within three years of writing it (Estates 3-2.2).

The problem with a holographic Will is its authenticity. Because no one saw the decedent sign the Will, it is hard to determine whether the Will was written by the decedent or is a forgery. If all the decedent left was a holographic Will, then you should consult with an attorney experienced in Probate matters.

Sometimes a person who is of sound mind, makes a Will, but that Will has the effect of giving a spouse or a minor child less than is required to receive under New York law. One such example is that of Nancy. Hers was not an easy life. She divorced her hard drinking first husband. The final judgment gave her their homestead, some securities and sole custody of their daughter, Anne. After the divorce, Nancy had her attorney prepare a Will leaving all she owned to Anne. She had the attorney change the deed to her name and Anne, as joint tenants.

Some years later Nancy met and married Harry. He moved into her home and they later had twin boys. Nancy never did get around to changing the Will once she remarried.

Anne was 18, and her stepbrothers 12, when Nancy died after a lengthy battle with cancer. Just before she died, Nancy gave Anne $10,000 because she wanted to be sure Anne had enough cash for her first semester of college.

Nancy did not have much when she died — the house, now worth $80,000, her furnishings, her car (worth $12,000) and securities and bank accounts worth about $40,000.

When the funeral was over, Harry discovered the Will (leaving all to Anne). He also found the cancelled $10,000 check, but the thing that sent him ballistic, was having Anne tell him that she was putting the house up for sale.

Harry went to his attorney.

"I was a good husband to Nancy, taking care of her right up to her death. Don't I have any rights? And what about my sons — don't they have any rights?"

"They sure do. New York law provides that if a child is born after a Will is made, then that child is entitled to inherit as much as his siblings. This means that whatever Anne inherits will be split three ways with all three children getting an equal share (Estates 5-3.2). As for your rights, New York law allows you to *waive* (give up) your rights in your spouse's estate (5-1.1 (f)). Did you sign a pre-nuptial or post-nuptial agreement giving up any or all of your rights?"

"Absolutely not!"

"In that case, New York law gives you the right to $50,000 or one third of your wife's *net estate* whichever is the greater value. The net estate consists of all of the property your wife owned including the homestead that she held jointly with Anne and the $10,000 she gave to her daughter in contemplation of her death. In addition, you are entitled to keep all of the household furnishing (up to $10,000 in value), money or other personal property (up to $15,000) and your wife's car (Estates 5-3.1)."

"Sounds good to me."

No doubt Nancy did not think that her Will would be challenged, but challenged it was. By the time the funeral expenses, medical bills, and the cost of probating the estate were paid, there was little left for Anne.

Had Nancy known about New York law, she could have consulted with an attorney and set up an estate plan that would have accomplished her goals. But, the moral of the story, for the purpose of this discussion, is that if you believe that the decedent's Will is not valid or is not drafted according to New York law, then you need to consult with an attorney experienced in probate matters to determine your legal rights under that Will.

Getting Possession Of The Property 6

Knowing who is entitled to receive the decedent's property is one thing. Getting that property is another. As explained in the previous chapter if the property is held jointly with someone, or in a trust for someone, then the property belongs to the joint owner or beneficiary. The joint owner or beneficiary is free to take possession of the property.

If the decedent held property in his name only, then some sort of probate procedure is necessary in order to transfer ownership to the proper beneficiary. Many of the probate procedures allowed by New York statute are relatively simple and can be done without the assistance of an attorney. You will need the counsel of an attorney, experienced in probate matters, for large estates or in cases where there is some problem, such as whether a valid Will exists, or whether a creditor has the right to be paid.

This chapter explains the various probate procedures and when it is appropriate to use that procedure.

DISTRIBUTING PERSONAL PROPERTY

Too often, the first person to discover the body will help himself to the decedent's *personal effects* (clothing, jewelry, appliances, electrical equipment, cameras, books, household items and furnishing, etc.). Unless that person is the decedent's sole beneficiary, such action is unconscionable, if not illegal.

If the decedent was married and did not have children, then all of the decedent's personal effects belong to his spouse. Even if the decedent had children, the spouse is entitled to all of the household furnishings and appliances up to $10,000 in value (see page 82). If the decedent was not married, then all of his personal effects should be given to the Personal Representative (or Executor) named in the decedent's Will. The Personal Representative then has the duty to distribute the property according to New York or as directed in the decedent's Will.

If there is no Will, then the next of kin need to determine whether the decedent left a list or written statement of how he wanted his personal property distributed. If the decedent left a written statement of how he wanted his personal effects distributed, then those wishes need to be respected.

If the decedent did not have a Will, and was not married, then his children are entitled to divide all of the personal effects among themselves in approximately equal proportions. If the decedent was single and without children, then the personal effects of the decedent are distributed according to New York's Rules Governing Intestate Succession. See Chapter 5 for an explanation of the law.

Most personal effects have little, if any, monetary value. Furniture may be worth less than it costs to move. In such case, the beneficiaries may decide to donate the personal property to the decedent's favorite charity. Of course, if the decedent owned some item of great value such as an antique or an expensive painting, then a formal probate procedure will be necessary before the asset can be distributed to the proper beneficiary.

WHAT'S EQUAL?

The decedent's Will or if no Will, then the Rules Of Intestate Succession may direct that the decedent's personal property be divided equally between two or more beneficiaries. The problem with the term "equal" is that people have different ideas of what "equal" means. Unless there is clear evidence that the decedent's Will meant something else, "equal" refers to the monetary value of the item and not to the number of items received. For example, to divide the decedent's personal effects equally, one beneficiary may receive an expensive item of jewelry and another beneficiary may receive several items whose overall value is approximately equal to that single piece of jewelry.

When distributing personal effects there needs to be cooperation and perhaps compromise, or else bitter arguments might arise over items of little monetary value. One such argument occurred when an elderly woman died who was rich only in her love for her five children and 12 grandchildren. After the funeral, the children gathered in their mother's apartment. Each child had his/her own furnishings and no need for anything in the apartment. They agreed to donate all of their mother's personal effects to a local charity with the exception of a few items of sentimental value.

Each child took some small item as a remembrance — a handkerchief, a large platter that their mother used to serve family dinners, a doily their mother crocheted. Things went smoothly until it came to her photograph album. Frank, the youngest sibling, said, "I'll take this." Marie objected saying, "But there are pictures in that album that I want." Frank retorted, "You already took all the pictures Mom had on her dresser."

The argument went downhill from there. Unsettled sibling rivalries boiled over, fueled by the hurt of the loss that they were all experiencing. It almost came to blows when the eldest settled the argument:

"Frank you make copies of all of the photos in the album for Marie. Marie, you make copies of all of the pictures that you took and give them to Frank. This way you both will have a complete set of Mom's pictures.

And while you're at it make copies for the rest of us."

TRANSFERRING THE CAR

If the decedent owned a motor vehicle, then title to the car needs to be transferred to the new owner and new owner needs to register the car in the state where it will be driven. You may want to limit the use of the car until it is transferred to the beneficiary. If the decedent's car is involved in an accident before the car is transferred to the new owner, then the decedent's estate may be liable for the damage. Having adequate insurance on the car may save the estate from monetary loss, but a pending lawsuit could delay the probate procedure and prevent any money from being distributed to the beneficiaries until the lawsuit is settled.

WHO IS ENTITLED TO THE CAR

As explained in chapter 5, if title to the car was held jointly, then the joint owner now owns the car. If the decedent was married and the value of the car does not exceed $15,000, then the spouse has the right to the car (see page 82). If the decedent was not survived by a spouse, but by children under the age of 21, then it goes to them.

If the decedent died testate and did not make a specific gift of the car in his Will, then the car goes to the *residuary beneficiaries* under his Will, i.e. to those people who inherit whatever is left after all gifts specified in the Will are made and all of the decedent's bills and costs of probate have been paid.

If the decedent died without a will and no surviving spouse and no child under the age of 21, then the car belongs to the decedent's heirs as determined by the New York's Rules of Intestate Succession (see page 102).

MORE THAN ONE BENEFICIARY

If there is more than one person who has the right to inherit the car, then the beneficiaries need to decide who will take title to the car. The person who takes title to the car may need to compensate the other heirs for their share of the car. If so, then they all need to come to an agreement as to the value of the car.

DETERMINING THE VALUE OF THE CAR

Cars are valued in many different ways. The *collateral* value of the car is the value that banks use to evaluate the car for purposes of making a loan to the owner of the car. Because banks print these values in book form, the collateral value is also referred to as the *book value* of the car. If you were to trade in a car for the purpose of purchasing a new car, then the car dealer will offer you the *wholesale* value of the car. Were you to purchase that same car from a car dealer, then he will price it at its *retail* or *fair market value*. Usually the retail price is highest, wholesale is lowest and the book value of the car is somewhere in between.

You can call your local bank to get the book value of the car. It may be more difficult to obtain the wholesale value of the car because the amount of money a dealer is willing to pay for the car depends on the value of the new car that you are purchasing. You can get some idea of the car's retail value by looking at comparable used car advertisements in the local newspaper.

 You can determine both wholesale and retail values of the car by using one or more of the search engines on the Internet to find web sites that will give both wholesale and retail car values.

LOCATE THE CERTIFICATE OF TITLE

To make the transfer you will need to turn in the certificate of title to the Motor Vehicle Division, together with a certified copy of the death certificate. If you cannot find the certificate of title, then you need to apply for a duplicate title at the Department of Motor Vehicle. There is a $10 fee to get a copy of the title. For information call:

Upstate New York: (800) 225-5368

From 516, 631 and 914 area codes: (800) 342-5368

Metropolitan New York: (212) 645-5550 or (718) 966-6155

For the hearing impaired: within state TDD (800) 368-1186

Once you obtain a copy of the certificate of title, you may discover that the title identifies a lienholder (lender). In such case, you need to contact the lender to obtain a copy of the promissory note and record of payments. You will not be able to transfer title to the car unless the lender gives written permission to do so. The lender will probably require payment in full before allowing the transfer. Some lenders will allow the beneficiary to take title to the car provided the beneficiary agrees to be responsible for the balance of payments.

It is relatively simple to transfer the decedent's motor vehicle. If the value does not exceed $15,000 and the decedent is survived by a spouse or child under 21, then the spouse, child (or guardian of the child) can make the transfer by signing their name in the transfer section of the title certificate followed by their relationship to the decedent, for example "RUBY LANE, spouse."

In addition, the person making the transfer must sign an *affidavit* (a sworn statement that the facts are true) in the presence of a notary public stating that:

☑ The spouse (or child) is the proper successor to the motor vehicle;

☑ The motor vehicle does not exceed $15,000 in value;

☑ The motor vehicle is the only vehicle being transferred according to Estates 5-3.1
(See Page 80 for a statement of the law).

The Department of Motor Vehicles will give you the affidavit form (MV-349.1)

If there is no Will, spouse or child under 21 and no probate procedure is necessary, then the next of kin can use form MV-349 to transfer title to the motor vehicle. The form contains an affidavit that must be signed in the presence of a notary public. Other members of the decedent's immediate family must consent to the transfer by signing the back of the form.

In all other cases, the Personal Representative must sign the transfer section of the title certificate, and also fill out the appropriate transfer form.

COMPLETING THE TRANSFER

The person inheriting the vehicle must fill out the sales tax exemption form (DTF-803). If someone is buying the car from the decedent's estate, then the sales tax form (DTF-802) needs to be completed. The new owner will need to pay registration and plate fees, and show a NYS insurance identification card.

Your local Department of Motor Vehicles will walk you through the process. It is best to first call them (see page 121 for the telephone numbers) and ask what documents you need to bring with you, and how much you will need to pay to make the transfer.

TRANSFERRING OTHER MOTOR VEHICLES

A mobile home is a motor vehicle, as is a boat, trailer and snowmobile. The same procedure can also be used to transfer these items. If you want to transfer the decedent's mobile home, then before doing so, you need to determine whether the land on which the mobile home is located was leased or owned by the decedent.

If the decedent was renting space in a trailer park, then you need to contact the trailer park owner to transfer the lease to the beneficiary of the mobile home. If the decedent owned the land under the mobile home, then a full probate procedure will be necessary to transfer the land to the proper beneficiary.

Special Situation ⟩ THE LEASED CAR

If the decedent's car was leased, then the car belongs to the lessor and the lessor has possession of the title certificate. Ask the lessor to give you a copy of the leasing contract. Once you have the contract, you can check to see whether the decedent took out life insurance as part of the agreement. If so, then upon his death the lease is paid in full. The next of kin or the Personal Representative can send the death certificate to the leasing company with a copy of the contract and a letter requesting that the paid contract be transferred to the beneficiary who can use the car for the remainder of the leasing period, or take title to the car, whichever option is available.

If there is no insurance to pay off the lease, the personal representative (or next of kin) needs to see to it that the person who will inherit the decedent's estate agrees to be liable for the remaining payments. If it happens that the remaining payments exceed the current market value of the car, there may be a temptation to hand the keys over to the leasing company. This may not be the best strategy. The thing to keep in mind is that the leasing contract is a liability to the decedent's estate and the leasing company is now a creditor of the estate.

If the decedent had no assets or if the only assets he had are creditor proof, then simply returning the car may be an option. But if the decedent's estate has assets available to pay the balance of the lease payments, then payments must be continued. If lease payments are not kept current, the lessor has the right to repossess the car AND sue the decedent's estate for the balance of the payments.

GETTING TAX REFUNDS

You need to file the decedent's final income tax return (IRS form 1040) by April 15th of the year following the year in which he died. If there is a refund due to the decedent and you are entitled to that money as the beneficiary of the decedent, then you can obtain the refund by filing IRS form 1310 along with the 1040. You can obtain this form 1310 from the decedent's accountant, or if he did not have an accountant and you wish to file yourself, then call the IRS at 1-800-829-3676 to obtain the proper form.

 IRS WEB SITE

You can obtain forms, instructions, and publications from the **INTERNAL REVENUE SERVICE** at the following web sites: **IRS FORMS AND INSTRUCTIONS**
http://www.irs.ustreas.gov/prod/forms_pubs/forms.html
IRS PUBLICATIONS
http://www.irs.ustreas.gov/prod/forms_pubs/pubs.html

If you are appointed as Personal Representative as part of a probate procedure, then you do not need to file form 1310 because once you file the decedent's final income tax return, any refund will be forwarded to you as Personal Representative. Similarly, a surviving spouse does not need to file form 1310 because the spouse will automatically receive any refund due on their joint income tax return.

STATE INCOME TAX REFUND

The decedent's final New York State income tax return needs to be filed at the same time the federal income tax return is filed. If the Personal Representative files the return, then any refund will be given to him to be deposited to the estate account.

If no probate procedure is necessary, then the next of kin can file the return. If there is a refund due, then the next of kin will need to complete a Survivor's Affidavit Form (AU 217). You can get the form from your accountant or you can call (800) 225-5829. You can also obtain the form from the New York State Income Tax Web Site (see page 61).

DEPOSITING THE TAX REFUND

If the tax refund check is sent to the Personal Representative, then he will deposit it the to estate account. If there is no probate procedure and the check is in the name of the decedent and you have a joint account with the decedent, then you can deposit to that account (see page 55).

If the refund check is in the name of the decedent and there is no joint account, then you can obtain that money by the using whatever probate procedure is appropriate, depending on the amount of the check and your relationship to the decedent.

The different probate procedures are explained on the next few pages.

TRANSFERRING PROPERTY BY AFFIDAVIT

New York statute (Surrogate's 1310) was designed to transfer certain personal property to the family of the decedent quickly and without the need for probate. Items that can be transferred under this statute are those items belonging to the decedent only, or to his estate, including:

✧ the decedent's last pay check

✧ the decedent's bank or securities account

✧ any of his personal property deposited with the medical examiner, nursing home, hospital, or similar agency

✧ any insurance benefit, pension or annuity payable to the decedent's estate

The amount that can be transferred, and when it can be transferred, depends on who is to receive the property:

⇨ Anytime after the death, up to $30,000, to the spouse.

⇨ At least 30 days after the death, up to $15,000 to the decedent's adult child, or parent, or brother or sister, or niece or nephew

⇨ At least 6 months after the death, up to $5,000 to anyone entitled to the property either by Will or intestate succession, or to someone who paid for the decedent's funeral expenses.

The spouse can get the property by submitting a certified copy of the death certificate and signing an affidavit that states that all of the property that the spouse is receiving by means of affidavit does not exceed $30,000. If the property is to go to a family member, then the family member (or surviving spouse) can get the property by signing an affidavit in the form described on page 128. If the property is to be transferred to anyone else, then the they can sign an affidavit in the form described on page 129.

AFFIDAVIT FOR TRANSFER OF PERSONAL PROPERTY
pursuant to Surrogate's Court Procedure 1310 (3)

Affiant declares that the following is true:

1. The decedent_____ (name)
died on_____ (date) at the county of _____
state of _____.

2. At least 30 days have elapsed since the date of death as shown in the certified copy of the death certificate of the decedent which is attached to this affidavit.

3. No fiduciary has qualified or been appointed to administer the decedent's estate.

4. The relationship of the affiant to the decedent is _____

5. The names and addresses of the persons entitled to and who will receive the money paid:_____
_____.

6. The following is a description of the property of the decedent that is to be paid, transferred, or delivered to those identified in paragraph 5:

_____

7. After diligent inquiry, Affiant states that this payment and all other payments made pursuant to Surrogate's Court Procedure 1310 (3) do not exceed $15,000.

I affirm or declare, under penalty of perjury under the laws of the State of New York, that the foregoing is true and correct.

Affiant Name _____
Affiant Signature _____ date_____
Affiant address:_____

Signed at _____ County, state of _____
_____
Notary Signature and Seal

When Someone Dies In New York

AFFIDAVIT FOR TRANSFER OF PERSONAL PROPERTY
pursuant to Surrogate's Court Procedure 1310 (4)

Affiant declares that the following is true:

1. The decedent _____(name)
died on_____ (date) at the county of _____
state of _____

2. At least 6 months have elapsed since the date of death as shown in the certified copy of the death certificate of the decedent which is attached to this affidavit.

3. No fiduciary has qualified or been appointed to administer the decedent's estate.

4. The decedent was not survived by spouse or minor child.

5. Affiant is entitled to the following property:

_____

6. After diligent inquiry, Affiant states that this payment and all other payments made pursuant to Surrogate's Court Procedure 1310 (4) do not exceed $5,000.

I affirm or declare, under penalty of perjury under the laws of the State of New York, that the foregoing is true and correct.

Affiant Name _____
Affiant Signature _____ date_____

Affiant address:_____

Signed at _____ County, state of _____

_____
Notary Signature and Seal

PROBATING THE SMALL ESTATE

The affidavit is appropriate to use if all the decedent left was a few thousand dollars, no debts to speak of, and all of the money going to one or two people. But suppose the decedent left a small amount of money and it goes to several people, or perhaps several of the decedent's creditors need to be paid. In that case, someone needs to take responsibility to settle the estate and then distribute whatever is left to the proper beneficiary. There is a relatively simple probate procedure designed to handle such situations. It is called a *Summary Procedure*.

To qualify for a Summary Procedure, the total amount of personal property to be transferred must not exceed $20,000, not counting all of the things that are exempt for the benefit of the family (see page 82). Someone needs to be appointed as *Voluntary Administrator* to settle the estate. If the decedent had a Will, then the Executor is entitled to be appointed. If the decedent died intestate, then the spouse has top priority for the appointment. If there is no spouse, or the spouse declines to serve, then an adult child or grandchild can serve as Voluntary Administrator. If none of these, then the decedent's parent, brother or sister, niece or nephew, aunt or uncle, in that order, can serve.

The position of Voluntary Administrator is one of trust. Whoever takes on the job does so without pay and without bond. Once the family agrees as to who is to serve as Voluntary Administrator, then that person needs to go to the Surrogate's Court in the county of the decedent's residence. If the decedent was not a resident of the state, then to the Surrogate's Court in the county where the personal property is located (Surrogate's 1301, 1302, 1303, 1304).

If you are going to be Voluntary Administrator, then you may save time by first calling the Clerk and asking:

How do I get to the courthouse?
When is the best time to meet with the Clerk?
What documents or information should I bring?
How much money will it cost?

You will need to sign an affidavit given to you by the Clerk. If someone has a higher priority to be appointed as Voluntary Administrator, then that person will need to agree, in writing, to your appointment. The Clerk will send out a post card telling those who have the right to inherit the decedent's property, that you have stated a Summary procedure.

Once the Clerk is satisfied that the estate qualifies for the Summary administration, he/she will give you a document called a **Short Certificate**. With the Short Certificate you will be able to get possession of the decedent's property. You will need to deposit all of the money you collect into a bank account that you open as Voluntary Administrator. You will pay all of the decedent's bills from this account, signing your name as Voluntary Administrator on all the checks. You will distribute whatever is left to the proper beneficiary. It is important that you do all this in an honest and conscientious manner, else the decedent's creditors and beneficiaries have the right to seek reimbursement from you for any error or wrongdoing.

Once you distribute the money, you need to report back to the Clerk with a full accounting of how much money you collected and to whom it was given.

THE FULL PROBATE PROCEDURE

If the decedent left real property or assets worth more than can be transferred by Affidavit or a Summary Procedure, then there needs to be a full Probate Procedure. The procedure can take anywhere from several months to more than a year depending on the size and complexity of the Probate Estate.

It is the Personal Representative's job to use the Probate Estate to pay all valid claims and then to distribute what is left to the proper beneficiary. All of the decedent's debts are paid from the Probate Estate and not from Personal Representative's pocket; but if the Personal Representative makes a mistake, then he may be responsible to pay for that mistake. For example, if he pays a debt that did not need to be paid — or if he transfers property to the beneficiaries too quickly and there were still taxes due on the estate, then he may be responsible to pay for the mistake (Estates 11-4.7).

The Personal Representative needs to employ an attorney to guide him through the process. It then becomes the job of the attorney for the Personal Representative to see to it that the estate is administered properly and without any personal liability to the Personal Representative. The cost of employing an attorney is a proper charge to the Probate Estate.

APPOINTING THE PERSONAL REPRESENTATIVE

The first step in the Probate procedure is to have someone appointed by the court as Personal Representative. If the decedent died testate, then whoever is named as Executor gets the job. If the decedent died intestate, then New York statute gives the order of priority for the job (see page 27).

A person cannot serve as Personal Representative if he is under the age of 18 or is a convicted felon. The judge can deny the appointment if the person is not a resident of the state of New York, or if he does not speak English, or he has a history of dishonesty or drug abuse (Surrogate's 707).

Of course the judge may not be aware of these flaws unless someone brings these things to his attention. If you feel strongly that the person with priority should not be appointed as Personal Representative, then you can file an objection prior to the time the person is appointed (Surrogate's 709).

You could file the objection on your own behalf, but if the person who has priority wants the appointment, then there could be a court battle on the issue. It is best to consult with an attorney of your choice to assist with the filing of the objection. As discussed, the attorney for the estate is employed by the Personal Representative, so if you have concerns, it is best to employ your own attorney.

If you lose the battle, you still have the right to ask that the court supervise the activities of the Personal Representative by giving him Letters that limit or restrict the things that he can do without court approval. For example, you could ask that the Personal Representative not be allowed to take sell certain of the decedent's assets without court approval (Surrogate's 702).

YOUR RIGHTS AS A BENEFICIARY

You, as a beneficiary, have the right to require that the Personal Representative keep you informed as to the progress of the probate procedure. If the estate is sizeable, then consider employing your own attorney to check that things are done properly and in a timely manner. If you are not in a financial position to employ an attorney, then you can take the following steps to protect you interests:

✧ REQUEST COPIES OF ALL DOCUMENTS

You have the right to receive a copy of documents filed with the court. If there is a Will, then you have the right to receive a copy of the Will. You have a right to receive a copy of the inventory of the estate assets. Write a letter to the attorney for the Personal Representative requesting copies of all documents filed with the court. Ask the attorney when you can expect to receive a copy of the inventory.

✧ DEMAND SUFFICIENT BOND

It doesn't happen often, but every now and again a Personal Representative will run off with estate funds. A bond is insurance for the estate. If estate monies are stolen, then the insurance company will reimburse the estate for the loss. New York law requires that the Personal Representative be bonded for the value of all personal property (stocks, bonds, bank accounts, etc.) The judge has the right to waive the bond, so you need to check to see that a bond has, in fact, been required. If not, you can ask the court to set bond equal to the value of all of the personal property. If monies are found after the bond value is set, then you have the right to ask the Court to increase the value of the bond (Surrogate's 801).

✧ DETERMINE FEES

The Personal Representative and his attorney have the right to charge the estate for their services (see Page 192 for the amount allowed by law). The money paid to the Personal Representative is taxable to him as ordinary income. If the Personal Representative is a beneficiary of the estate he may decide not to charge for his services, because any money paid to him, is just that much less he will inherit. The amount he inherits is not taxable as ordinary income, so he may find it better to charge little or no fee.

Ask the Personal Representative whether he intends to charge a fee. Have him put the response in writing, even if his reply is that he will not charge a fee. If the Personal Representative says that he has not made up his mind, then ask him to let you know of his decision as soon as possible.

Ask the Personal Representative to give you a copy of the retainer agreement that he signed with his attorney, so that you will know how much is being charged for legal fees. If the attorney is employed on an hourly basis, have the attorney give a written estimate of the time he expects to expend on the probate procedure.

✧ REQUIRE A FULL ACCOUNTING

Before the estate is closed, the Personal Representative should give each residuary beneficiary a full accounting. The accounting should show that taxes have been paid and all outstanding bills settled. If the Personal Representative tries to distribute money to the beneficiaries and/or close out the estate without first giving an accounting, then you have the right to ask the court to order that the Personal Representative provide that accounting (Surrogate's 2203 and 2205)

✧ GET PROOF OF PAYMENT OF TAXES & DEBTS

It is important that you receive copies of all tax returns that the Personal Representative is obliged to file. If the Personal Representative fails to file a return, or fails to pay taxes, or if he under reports a tax obligation, then you could later be called on to pay estate taxes out of the proceeds that you receive.

✧ IT'S YOUR RIGHT - DON'T BE INTIMIDATED

You may feel uncomfortable being assertive with a friend or family member who is Personal Representative. Don't be. It's your money and your legal right to be kept informed. Be especially firm if the Personal Representative waives you off with:

"You've known me for years. Surely you trust me."

People who are trustworthy, don't ask to be trusted. They do what is right. The very fact that the Personal Representative is resisting is a red flag. In such cases you can explain that it is not a matter of trust, but a matter of what is your legal right.

If you are still getting an argument, then close the discussion with "I am prepared to bring this matter to the attention of the court" and then call a lawyer.

HOW TO GET THE CONTENTS
OF THE SAFE DEPOSIT BOX

If the decedent leased a safe deposit box together with another person, each with full authority to enter the box, then the co-lessee of the box can remove all of its contents; but that may not be possible if the bank learned of the death and sealed the box. If the decedent was the sole lessee of the safe deposit box, then a probate procedure is necessary in order to get possession of the contents of the box.

If there is a full probate procedure, then a Personal Representative will be appointed by the Probate court. The court will issue Letters giving the Personal Representative authority to take possession of the decedent's assets. The Personal Representative can present the Letters to the bank or safe deposit box lessor, and they will give the Personal Representative access to the box and all of its contents.

Whether the contents of the box can be removed by Affidavit or by a Voluntary Administrator with a Short Certificate depends on the value of the estate. Both of these procedures require that the estate be less than a given value; so the first issue to deal with is the value of the contents of the box. If you believe that the contents of the box exceed the amount allowed under these procedures, then you need to consult with an attorney to assist you with a full probate procedure.

If you believe that the contents of the box are nominal, then it will still take a court order before you will be allowed to examine the contents of the box. To get the order, go to the Clerk of the Surrogate's Court in the county of the decedent's residence. If the decedent was not a resident of New York, then go to the Surrogate's Court in the county where the bank is located.

The Clerk of the Surrogate's Court should be able to help you to get that order — or at least point you in the right direction. Once you have the order you can remove the Will, any insurance policy and the deed to the burial plot. If the box contains other items, then ask the bank to make an inventory of the contents of the safe deposit box for you to give to the court.

The next step is to determine the value of the contents of the box. If there is jewelry in the box, you will not be able to take the jewelry out to get it appraised, so you may be forced to go through a full probate procedure in order to get the jewelry.

If the box contains coins or stock or other items that can be easily evaluated, and if that value (plus any other item to be transferred) qualifies for a Summary Procedure, then you can use that procedure to get possession of the contents of the box. You will need to take the inventory prepared by the bank to the Surrogate's Court when you start the Summary Procedure. Once you have the Short Certificate, you can present it to the bank and they will give the contents of the box.

If the contents of the box can be transferred by an Affidavit, then you can offer that document to the bank officials. It may be that the bank will want the court to authorize the withdrawal. In such case, you may need to go through a Summary Procedure and give them a Short Certificate before they allow you to empty the box.

THE CHECK LIST

We have discussed many things that need to be done when someone dies in the state of New York. There is a check list on the next page that you may find helpful.

You can check those items that you need to do, and then cross them off the list once they are done. We made the list as comprehensive as possible, so many items may not apply in your case. In such case, you can cross them off the list or mark them *N/A* (not applicable).

Things to do

FUNERAL ARRANGEMENTS TO BE MADE
- [ ] AUTOPSY   [ ] ANATOMICAL GIFT
- [ ] DISPOSITION OF BODY OR ASHES

DEATH CERTIFICATE
- [ ] RECORD WITH COUNTY RECORDER

GIVE COPY TO: _____

_____

NOTICE OF DEATH

PEOPLE TO BE NOTIFIED _____

COMPANIES TO NOTIFY
- [ ] TELEPHONE COMPANY
  - [ ] LOCAL CARRIER   [ ] LONG DISTANCE   [ ] CELLULAR
- [ ] NEWSPAPER (OBITUARY PRINTED)
- [ ] NEWSPAPER CANCELLED   [ ] deposit refund
- [ ] SOCIAL SECURITY
- [ ] INTERNET SERVER
- [ ] TELEVISION CABLE COMPANY
- [ ] NEW YORK POWER & LIGHT   [ ] deposit refund
- [ ] POST OFFICE
- [ ] OTHER UTILITIES (GAS, WATER)   [ ] deposit refund
- [ ] PENSION PLAN
- [ ] ANNUITY
- [ ] HEALTH INSURANCE COMPANY
- [ ] LIFE INSURANCE COMPANY
- [ ] HOME INSURANCE COMPANY
- [ ] MOTOR VEHICLE INSURANCE COMPANY
- [ ] CONDOMINIUM OR HOMEOWNER ASSOCIATION
- [ ] CANCEL SERVICE CONTRACT   [ ] deposit refund
- [ ] CREDIT CARD COMPANIES _____

_____

_____

Things to do

REMOVE DECEDENT AS BENEFICIARY OF:
- ☐ WILL
- ☐ INSURANCE POLICY
- ☐ PENSION PLAN
- ☐ BANK OR IRA ACCOUNT
- ☐ SECURITY

DEBTS

PAY DECEDENT'S DEBTS (AMOUNT & CREDITOR)

_____

COLLECT MONIES OWED TO DECEDENT (AMOUNT & DEBTOR)

_____

TAXES
- ☐ FILE FINAL FEDERAL INCOME TAX RETURN
- ☐ FILE FINAL NY STATE INCOME TAX RETURN
- ☐ RECEIVE INCOME TAX REFUND
- ☐ FILE ESTATE TAX RETURN

PROPERTY TO BE TRANSFERRED
- ☐ PERSONAL EFFECTS
- ☐ MOTOR VEHICLE
- ☐ BANK ACCOUNT
- ☐ CREDIT UNION ACCOUNT
- ☐ IRA ACCOUNT
- ☐ SECURITIES
- ☐ BROKERAGE ACCOUNT
- ☐ INSURANCE PROCEEDS
- ☐ HOMESTEAD
- ☐ TIME SHARE
- ☐ OTHER REAL PROPERTY
- ☐ CONTENTS OF SAFE DEPOSIT BOX

OTHER THINGS TO DO

_____
_____
_____

Preneed Arrangements 7

Death is a wake-up call because once someone close to us dies we are reminded of our own mortality. We realize that death can be put off, but the inevitable is inevitable. Although we cannot change the fact of our death, we have the power to control the circumstances of our death by making preneed arrangements.

You can make preneed arrangements so that you will be buried in the manner you wish and where you wish. You can also make arrangements that direct the kind of medical treatments you want to be given in the event you become seriously ill.

You can legally appoint someone to make your medical decisions in the event that you are too ill to speak for yourself. If you let that person know how you feel about life support systems, autopsies and anatomical gifts, then that person will be authorized to act on your behalf and will see to it that your wishes are carried out.

As this chapter will show, it is relatively simple and inexpensive to make such preneed arrangements.

MAKING BURIAL ARRANGEMENTS

When making burial arrangements for the decedent, you may decide to purchase one or more burial spaces nearby for yourself or other family members.

If the decedent was buried in the family plot, then this is the time to take inventory of the number of spaces left and who in the family expects to use those spaces.

If all of the spaces are taken and if you plan to be cremated, then as explained in Chapter 1, some cemeteries will allow an urn to be placed in an occupied family plot. You can call the cemetery and ask them to explain their policy as it relates to the burial of an urn in a currently occupied grave site or mausoleum.

If this is not an option, and the cemetery of your choice has a columbarium, you might consider purchasing a space at this time.

If you wish to have your cremains scattered, then you need to let your next of kin know where and how this is to be done.

VETERAN OR
VETERAN'S SPOUSE

If you are an honorably discharged veteran, you have the right to be buried in a Veterans National Cemetery. You cannot reserve a grave site in advance. If your Veteran spouse was buried in a Veterans National Cemetery, then you have the right to be buried in that same grave site unless soil conditions require a separate grave site.

If you wish to be buried in a Veterans National Cemetery, then check on current availability (see page 17 for telephone numbers). Let your next of kin know your choice of cemetery.

To establish your eligibility your next of kin will need to provide the following information:

➤   the veteran's rank, serial, social security
    and VA claim numbers

➤   the branch of service; the date and place of
    entry into and separation from the service

The next of kin will also need to provide the VA with a copy of the veteran's official military discharge document bearing an official seal or a DD 214 form.

If you wish to be buried in a national cemetery, then make all of these items readily accessible to your family.

MAKING FUNERAL ARRANGEMENTS

If you are financially able, in addition to purchasing a burial space, consider purchasing a Preneed funeral plan. It will be easier on your family emotionally and financially if you make your own funeral arrangements. If you do not have sufficient cash on hand for the kind of funeral you desire, then many funeral directors offer an installment payment plan.

Once you decide on a plan, the funeral director will present you with a contract. The print may be small, but it is worth your effort to read it before signing. If the contract is written in "legalese," then either consult with your attorney before signing it or ask as many questions of the funeral director as is necessary to make the terms of the contract clear to you. If you are not satisfied with the way a certain section of the contract is written, then add an addendum to the contract that explains, in plain English, your understanding of that passage.

If you are concerned about something that is not mentioned in the contract, then insist that the contract be amended to include that item, for example:

Does the contract cover all costs?
The contract should contain an itemized list stating exactly what goods and services are included in the sales price. Ask the funeral director whether there will be any additional cost when you die. For example, if you have not purchased a burial space, then that cost needs to be factored in.

Some funeral directors offer combination funeral and burial plans, namely contracts that include the cost of a burial space. Other contracts are for the funeral only. If you made provision for a burial space, then you need to make the funeral director aware of where you have arranged to be buried. If you have not made provision, then the funeral director can assist you in making burial arrangements.

What if you die in another state or country?

It is a good idea to have the contract spell out what provision will be made in the event that you move to another state or in the event you happen to die in another state or country. Many funeral firms are part of a national funeral service corporation with funeral firms located throughout the United States, so this is not usually a problem.

How are your contract funds protected?

New York laws are designed to protect the purchaser of a Preneed funeral plan. Funeral firms are required to protect funds paid by the consumer of a Preneed funeral plan by placing the funds in an interest bearing trust account within 10 days of receipt. The funeral firm is required to notify the purchaser, in writing, within 30 days, that the funds have been deposited and the location of the bank. Each year, the funeral firm must give the purchaser a statement of the location of the account and the annual interest earned on that account (General Business 453).

Should the funeral firm go out of business, then the firm must, within 30 days, repay all of the monies, together with the earned interest. If the firm is sold, then the new owner must notify the purchaser of the sale, and of the location and amount in the trust account (Public Health 3442). Check to see whether the contract reflects these New York laws.

Of course all of these safeguards may fail if you are not doing business with a reputable funeral home. It is prudent to take the time to call the New York Bureau of Funeral Directing at (518) 402-0785. Ask whether the funeral home is licensed and if any complaints have been filed against them.

Can you cancel the contract?
New York statute gives the purchaser of a Preneed contract the right to cancel the entire contract at any time and receive a full refund together with any interest earned on the trust account (General Business 453 (2))

New York statute allows an ***irrevocable*** contract (one that can't be cancelled) to be sold to people who are applying for, or receiving, Medicaid, Supplemental Security Income ("SSI") or certain Social Services. These programs have limits on the amount of assets owned by an applicant. New York law allows irrevocable contracts to be sold to people in these programs so as not to have the funeral contract affect their eligibility to qualify for the program (General Business 453 (1b)). If you purchase a contract and then later need to apply for any of these programs, you can have the funeral firm change the contract to one that is irrevocable.

Can the plan be changed?

New York law is clear that the purchaser of a Preneed plan has the right to cancel the contract, but what if his heirs need (or want) to do so? Certainly you would want the Preneed funds given to your heirs in any unusual situation such as:

➤ a missing body or one that cannot be recovered
➤ burial by another facility because your heirs were unaware of your Preneed contract
➤ burial in another country

New York law requires that, if your agreement does not provide for a change in price, then the funeral firm must deliver the goods and services at the agreed upon contract price (General Business 453 (3e(iii)). But what if your heirs decide on a plan different than the one you purchased? Would you want them to be able to purchase a more expensive plan and pay the difference?

Would you want your heirs to be able to change to a lesser plan and receive a refund?

If you are concerned that you get the exact type of funeral that you want, with no changes, except for certain extraordinary circumstances (i.e., a missing body) then have your contract with the funeral firm clearly state that no changes are to be made.

You may wonder why anyone would think of changing the decedent's funeral plan, but consider that in today's market, it is not uncommon for a Preneed contract to cost several thousand dollars. A top end funeral complete with solid bronze casket can cost upwards of $40,000.

And there may be other motivations. Consider the case of Mona, a difficult woman with a personality that can only be described as "sour." Her husband deserted her after four years of marriage leaving her to raise their son, Lester, by herself. Once Lester was grown, Mona made it clear to him that she had done her job and now he was on his own.

Lester could have used some help. He married and had three children. One of his children suffered with asthma and it was a constant struggle to keep up with the medical bills.

Mona believed in being good to herself. She did not intend to, nor did she, leave much money when she died. She knew that Lester would not be able to afford a "proper" burial for her, so she purchased a Preneed funeral plan and paid close to $15,000 for it. She was pleased when the funeral director told her that the monies would be kept safely in a local bank until the time they were needed.

When Mona died Lester asked an attorney at the Legal Aid office to determine whether the Preneed contract was revocable.

It was.

You know the ending to this story.

PURCHASING BURIAL INSURANCE

Instead of purchasing a Preneed funeral plan, you might consider purchasing a life insurance policy payable to your estate with instructions to your Executor that the money from this policy is to be used to purchase a funeral plan as directed in your Will. The cost of the policy might be less than purchasing a Preneed plan. You could insure yourself with sufficient monies to cover the cost of the burial and other miscellaneous expenses such as paying for dinner after the burial, or paying the airfare for a family member to attend the service.

If you wish to purchase burial insurance, but you do not want to trigger a probate procedure for a single insurance policy, then you could name a trusted family member as the beneficiary of the policy. It is important that the person who is to receive the insurance funds clearly understands why he/she is named as beneficiary of the policy. It is equally important that the beneficiary agree to use the monies for the intended purpose.

It isn't so much that a family member is not trustworthy as it is that they may not understand what you intended — especially in those cases where other estate funds may be available to pay for the funeral. Too often insurance funds are left to a sibling who then refuses to contribute to the cost of the funeral saying in effect "Dad wanted me to have this money — that's why he left it to me."

To avoid a misunderstanding, put it in writing. It need not be a formal contract. It could be something as simple as a letter to the insurance beneficiary, with copies to your next of kin, saying something like:

Dear Romita,

I purchased a $10,000 insurance policy today naming you as beneficiary of the policy. As we discussed this money is to be used to pay for the following:
- my funeral and grave site
- my headstone
- perpetual care for my grave
- airfare for each of my grandchildren to attend the funeral
- dinner for the family after the wake
- lunch for the family after the funeral

If there is any money left over, please accept it as my thanks for all the effort spent on my behalf.

Love,
  Dad

P.S. I am sending a copy of this letter to your brother so that he will know that all arrangements have been made.

Whether or not you arrange to pay for your burial or funeral, you need to let your next of kin know your feelings about the burial procedure. Let your family know whether you wish to be cremated or buried. If you wish to have a religious service, then let your family know the type of service and where it is to be held. Let the family know where you wish to be buried, or if you intend to be cremated, then where to place the ashes.

AUTOPSIES

As discussed in Chapter 1, some autopsies are optional. If you have strong feelings about allowing an optional autopsy or not allowing the procedure, then let your family know how you feel.

ANATOMICAL GIFTS

If you wish to make an anatomical gift, you can make that donation by completing a donor card. The Department of Motor Vehicles will provide you with the form and they will indicate, on your driver's license, that you have signed a donor card (Vehicle & Traffic 504).

If you are aged, and in poor health, the local Organ Procurement Organization will probably not consider your body for transplantation of body parts, but you can still donate your body for education and research. If you wish to make such as donation, call or write to a local school of medicine (see page 6). They will forward a Dedication Form to you along with information on the subject.

If you do not wish to make an anatomical gift, then let your family know how you feel.

Of course, there are problems with just telling someone how you feel about your burial arrangements, autopsies, and anatomical gifts:

YOU TELL THE WRONG PERSON

The person you confide in may not be present when the arrangements are made. For example, if you tell your spouse what arrangements to make then he/she may die before you do — or you could die simultaneously in a car or plane crash.

You may tell someone who does not have authority to carry out your wishes. That was the case with James. Once his wife died, he moved to a retirement community where he lived for 15 years until his death. James had two sons who lived in different states. Although he loved his sons, he had difficulty talking to either of them about serious matters. It was easier for him to talk with his buddies in the retirement community. They often spoke about dying and how they felt about different burial arrangements. James often reminisced about his youth and growing up in a farming community in the plains state of Kansas. "I was happy and free. Out there you had room to breathe. It would be nice to be buried there — peaceful and spacious."

When he died, his friends told his sons about their father's desire to be buried in Kansas. They met the suggestion with scepticism and pragmatism:
"Dad didn't say anything like that to me."
"It would cost us double, if we had to arrange for burial in another state. I'm sure he didn't have that kind of expense in mind."

THE PERSON DOES NOT CARRY OUT YOUR WISHES

The person you tell may not understand what you said or perhaps they hear only what they want to hear. An example that comes to mind is the mother who constantly complained that she felt like a burden to her children. She would often say "When I die, just burn my body and throw my ashes out to sea." Her children paid no attention. When she died she was given a full funeral and buried in a local cemetery. They never asked, nor did they consider, that their mother might really have wanted to have her ashes spread out to sea.

WHO WANTS TO TALK ABOUT IT?

For many people the main problem with telling someone what to do when you die is talking about your death. It may be an uncomfortable, if not unpleasant, subject for you to bring up, and for your family to discuss. If this is the case, then consider putting the information in writing and give the instructions to the person who will have the job of carrying out your wishes.

PREPARING A HEALTH CARE PROXY

You can legally appoint someone to carry out your wishes relating to the care of your person, both before and after death, by signing a document called a *Health Care Proxy*. The proxy appoints a *Health Care Agent* to make your medical decisions in the event that you are too ill to speak for yourself. The Health Care Proxy can include a *Living Will* i.e., a statement that you do (or do not) wish life support systems to be used in the event that you are dying and there is no hope for your recovery.

There is a statutory form of the Health Care Proxy that you can use to appoint a Health Care Agent. You can find the form in the New York Consolidated Statutes (Public Heath 2981 (4)). The statutes can be found in most Public Libraries and in the Courthouse library. You can download the statutory form of the Health Care Proxy from the New York Statute web site:

 NEW YORK STATUTE WEB SITE
http://assembly.state.ny.us/ALIS

You can use the statutory forms as a basis and then add any provision you wish relating to autopsies, anatomical gifts and funeral arrangements. For the Health Care Proxy to be legally binding, you need to sign it as directed in the statute, namely in the presence of two witnesses, neither of whom are the person you are appointing as your Health Care Agent.

New York law allows a Do-Not-Resuscitate order which is an order given by a physician directing the hospital staff not to attempt to revive the patient in the event that the patient stops breathing or his heart stops beating. The order is given in situations where the patient is terminally ill and such medical procedures would only serve to prolong the dying process. The order may only be given after the physician consults with another physician and they both agree, in writing, that efforts to resuscitate the patient would be futile. They must also get the permission from the patient or his Health Care Agent to issue the order.

If the patient did not appoint a Health Care Agent, then they will seek permission from the following people:

1st	a court appointed guardian, if any
2nd	the spouse
3rd	a child who is 18 or older
4th	a parent
5th	a brother or sister who is 18 or older
6th	a close friend

A person with priority must be reasonably available, willing and competent to act. If not, the next one with priority will make the decision (Public Health 2965 (2)).

If this order of priority is not as you wish, or if there is someone you wish to exclude altogether from making your health care decisions, then it is important to sign a Health Care Proxy and appoint the person of your choice to act as your Health Care Agent.   If not, life decisions made for you, may not be as you would have wished.

George is a case in point. His wife became ill with Alzheimer's disease. He cared for her at home for as long as he was able, but finally, it was too much for him. He placed her in a local nursing facility. He and his two daughters visited her frequently, even though she scarcely recognized them. Emily's husband also suffered from Alzheimer's disease and was at the same facility.

George and Emily met at the nursing home support group and found that they had much in common. After visiting with their respective spouses they would go to the local coffee shop. One thing led to another, and soon they were an item.

George's daughters were not happy with the coupling. They criticized everything about Emily, from the way she dressed to her table manners. When Emily moved in with George, his daughters made cutting remarks about Emily's moral character.

Emily didn't take it personally. She believed the girls were more concerned about their inheritance than George's happiness. A second marriage might cut into what they already considered to be rightfully theirs.

Not that George and Emily planned to wed. They both loved their respective spouses and had no intention of trying to obtain a divorce. Their understanding was that if and when they both were single, they would discuss marriage at that time.

George and Emily were most compatible. Their affection for each other increased over the years. Each was happier than they had ever been before, until the day of the accident. George had a stroke while driving a car. His suffered serious injuries and lapsed into a coma. The prognosis was not encouraging. The doctors said George's heart was failing and he was having difficulty breathing. They could put him on a ventilator, but even using heroic measures, there was little hope that he would survive. And if he did live, the stroke was so damaging that it was doubtful he would regain consciousness.

Emily pleaded to keep him alive. "Let's try everything. If he doesn't improve we can always discontinue life support systems later."

George's daughters did not see it that way. "Why torture him with electric shocks, needles and breathing tubes? Let him pass on peacefully."

George never signed a Living Will so no one knew whether he would have wanted life support systems to be applied. He never signed a Health Care Proxy to appoint someone to make his medical decisions in the event he was unable to do so. In the absence of a Health Care Proxy the doctors had no choice but to consult with his daughters. Under New York law, the daughters were 3rd in priority. Emily was 6th.

The Do-Not-Resuscitate Order was signed.

George died.

Everyman's Estate Plan 8

The first six chapters of this book describe how to wind up the affairs of the decedent. As you read those chapters, you learned about the kinds of problems that can occur when someone dies. It is relatively simple for you to make an estate plan so that your family members are not burdened with similar problems. An *estate plan* is the arranging of one's finances to reduce (if not eliminate) probate costs and estate taxes, so that your beneficiaries inherit your property quickly and at little cost.

If you think that only wealthy people need to prepare an estate plan, you are mistaken. Each year, heirs of relatively modest estates, spend thousands of dollars to settle an estate. A bit of planning could have eliminated most, if not all, of the hassle and cost suffered by those families.

The suggestions in this chapter are designed to assist the average person in preparing a practical and inexpensive estate plan, so we have named this chapter EVERYMAN'S ESTATE PLAN. Once you create your own estate plan, you can rest assured that your family will not be left with more problems than happy memories of you.

AVOIDING PROBATE

Probate procedures can be costly and time consuming. If you have a small estate and only one or two beneficiaries, then it is not all that difficult to arrange your finances so that there will be no need for probate when you die.

BANK ACCOUNTS

You can arrange to have all of your bank accounts, including certificates of deposit, titled so that the money goes directly to your heirs when you die. For example, suppose all you have is a bank account with a balance of $50,000 and you want to have this go to your son and daughter when you die. You might think that a simple solution is to put each child's name on the account, but consider the ramifications of a joint account:

THE JOINT ACCOUNT

A joint bank account gives each joint owner of the account complete access to that account. If you hold the account jointly with your children, then each child can write a check on that account, the same as yourself. When you die the remaining joint owner (or joint owners) can withdraw all of the money from the account. There are potential problems with this arrangement:

⊠ POTENTIAL LIABILITY

If you hold property jointly with one of your adult children and that child is sued or gets a divorce then the child may need to disclose their ownership of the joint account. In such a case, you may find yourself spending money to prove that the account was established to avoid probate and that all of the money in that account really belongs to you.

⊠ THE MINOR CHILD

New York law gives a minor the right to be the owner of a bank account, or a securities account and even the right to lease a safe deposit box (Banking 239, 334, 6024); but if you elect a minor as the joint owner of your account, would you want the child to have the ability to remove money from your account. If you die, would you want the minor to be able to go to the bank and withdraw all of the money?

⊠ OVERREACHING

If you set up a joint account with your child so that the child has authority to withdraw funds from the account, then funds may be withdrawn without your authorization. If you open a joint account with two of your children, then after your death the first child to the bank may decide to withdraw all of the money and that will, at the very least, cause hard feelings between them.

Because of these inherent problems, you might want to hold the funds so that your beneficiary does not gain access to the monies until and unless you die. That can be done by setting up a trust bank account.

THE TRUST ACCOUNT

You can set up a trust account with a financial institution (bank, savings and loan, credit union, etc.) and direct the financial institution to hold your account *in trust for* one or more beneficiaries that you name. Once you die, the beneficiary is given the trust funds (Estates 7-5.2 (4)). The beneficiary does not have access to that account during your lifetime so the trust account does not have the potential problems of the joint account.

GIFT FOR THE MINOR

If you set up a trust account for a minor, then should you die before the child reaches 18, and the amount in the account is $10,000 or less, then the funds will be given to the child's parents upon their request. The parent is required to use the funds for the benefit of the child. If the amount in the trust account exceeds $10,000, then the funds must either remain in the account until the child reaches 18, or if the parents want to withdraw the monies, the Surrogate's court will need to appoint a guardian to take control of the monies (Estates 7-5.3).

Guardianship procedures are expensive to establish and maintain, so the better route may be to utilize the NEW YORK UNIFORM TRANSFERS TO MINORS ACT. This law gives the owner of a bank account the right to name a person or a financial institution to be custodian of an account in the event that the owner dies before the beneficiary of the account reaches 21.   For example, suppose Patricia Barry wants to hold a bank account in trust for her minor child Frank Barry.   She can appoint the bank as custodian of the account in the event that she dies before Frank is 21, in the following manner:

Friendly Bank as Custodian for Frank Barry, Jr. under the NEW YORK UNIFORM TRANSFERS TO MINORS ACT.

Patricia is free to add or withdraw from the account during her lifetime. Once she dies, whatever remains in the account will be given to the Friendly Bank as custodian. If Frank is 21 or older, the bank will give him the money. If he is not yet 21, the bank will hold the money for him until his 21st birthday. If Patricia wishes, she can instruct the bank to deliver the proceeds of the account when Frank is 18 instead of 21 (Estates 7-6.3, 7-6.20, 7-6.21, 7-6.25).

If Patricia dies while Frank is a minor, the bank has the duty to take control of the account, and then manage and reinvest the monies in a prudent manner. The bank can deliver or spend as much of the money for Frank's care as they think advisable. If there is a disagreement about using the funds, then Frank's parent or guardian (or Frank himself if he is 14 or older) can ask a court to order the bank to use monies for Frank's care (Estates 7-6.12, 7-6.14).

The same law can be used to transfer securities, life insurance policies, even real property to a minor. The custodian does have the right to charge a reasonable fee for their efforts, so you need to check with the custodian to find out how they intend to manage the property and the estimated cost of doing so (Estates 7-6.9, 7-6.15)

REAL PROPERTY

As explained in Chapter 5, if you own real property together with another, then who will own the property upon your death depends on how the Grantee (or Party of the Second Part) is identified on the face of the deed. If you compare the Grantee clause of the deed to the examples on pages 93 through 98 you can determine who will inherit that property should you die. If you are not satisfied with the way the property will be inherited, then you need to consult with an attorney to change the deed so that it will conform to your wishes.

If you own the property in your name only, or as a Tenant-In-Common with another, then once you die, there will need to be a probate procedure to determine the proper beneficiary of that parcel of land. If your main objective is to avoid probate, then you can have an attorney change the deed so that once you die, the property descends to your beneficiary without the need for probate. But before you make a real estate transfer be it joint interest or life estate, you need to consider the downside of the transfer:

☒   LOSS OF INDEPENDENCE
You can have your deed changed so that you and a beneficiary are joint owners of the property or you can change title so that you have a life estate interest, meaning you have the right to live in the house until you die at which time the beneficiary owns the property, outright. Either of these options avoid probate of the property but you will not be able to sell that property during your lifetime without the beneficiary's permission. And if the beneficiary gives permission and the property is sold, the beneficiary will have the legal right to receive some portion of the proceeds of the sale.

Some people think it a good idea to simply transfer their homestead to a child, with the understanding that the parent(s) will continue to live there. But this just creates a new set of problems:

⊠   LOSS OF CREDITOR PROTECTION
Only $10,000 of your homestead is protected from creditors (see page 81), but you know your own finances and no doubt you have managed your affairs so that your homestead is secure from creditors. If you transfer your homestead to a child and he/she does not occupy that property as their homestead, then there is no creditor protection whatsoever. Your homestead could be lost if the child runs into serious financial difficulties or if the child gets sued. This is especially a risk if your child is a professional — doctor, nurse, accountant, financial planner, attorney, etc. If your child is found to be personally liable for damages, then the house could become part of the settlement of that law suit.

If your child is (or gets) married, then this complicates matters even more so. If the child gets divorced, the property will certainly be included as part of settlement agreement. This may be to your child's detriment because the child may need to share the value of the property with his ex-spouse. If you do not transfer the property, then it cannot become part of the marital equation.

⊠   POSSIBLE LOSS OF GOVERNMENT BENEFITS

If you transfer property, then depending upon the value of the transfer, you could be disqualified from receiving Medicaid or Supplemental Security Income ("SSI") benefits for up to 3 years from the date of transfer. The federal and state rules that determine the period of ineligibility are complex. If nursing care may be an issue in the future, then it is best to consult with an Elder Law attorney to prepare a Medicaid Estate Plan.

POTENTIAL TAX PROBLEMS

Before you make a real estate transfer be it joint interest, life estate or outright gift, you need to consider the tax consequences of the transfer:

⊠   POSSIBLE CAPITAL GAINS TAX

If you gift your homestead to your child and continue to live there until you die, then when the child sells the property there might be a capital gains tax. The child will be taxed on the increase in value from the day you bought the property. If you don't transfer your home and the child inherits the property, he/she inherits it at the market value as of your date of death. The child can sell the property at that time without any tax consequence.

⊠   POSSIBLE GIFT TAX

If the value of the transfer is worth more than $10,000 you need to file a gift tax return. For most of us, this is not a problem because no gift tax needs to be paid unless the value of the property (plus the value of all gifts in excess of $10,000 that you gave over your lifetime) exceed the estate tax credit (see the schedule on page 36.) But if you are in that tax bracket, then you need to be aware that you are "using up" your tax credit.

 **☎ LAWYER** OUT OF STATE PROPERTY

Each state is in charge of the way property located in that state is transferred. If you own property in another state (or country), then you need to consult with an attorney in that state (or country) to determine how that property will be transferred to your beneficiaries once you die. Most state laws are similar to New York, namely, property held as JOINT TENANTS WITH RIGHTS OF SURVIVORSHIP or a LIFE ESTATE INTEREST goes to your beneficiary without the need for probate.

If you own property in another state in your name only, or as a TENANT IN COMMON, or if you hold property jointly with your spouse in a community property state, then a probate procedure will probably need to be held in that state. If it is necessary for your heirs to have probate procedure in New York, then they will need an ancillary (secondary) procedure in the state in which the property is located. This may have the effect of doubling the cost of probate to your heirs.

Still another problem is the matter of taxes. New York's Estate taxes are tied to the Federal Estate tax. If your estate is too small to pay Federal Estate taxes (see page 36 for the schedule), then you pay no New York Estate tax. This may not be the case with other states, so in addition to paying extra for the second probate procedure, your heirs may need to pay Estate taxes in the state where the property is located. In such cases, you may wish to consult with an attorney for suggestions about how to set up your estate plan to avoid these problems.

A TRUST MAY BE THE SOLUTION (or not)

As we have seen, many of the ways to avoid probate involve methods with undesirable trade-offs. One way to avoid some of these potential problems is to set up a trust. If you have substantial assets, then you probably have heard this suggestion from your financial planner or attorney, or accountant. Even people of fairly modest means are being encouraged by these professionals to use a trust as the basis of their estate plan. But even trusts have their downside. But before getting into that, let's first discuss what a trust is and how it works:

SETTING UP A TRUST

To create a trust, an attorney prepares the trust document in accordance with the client's needs and desires. The person who signs the document is referred to as the *Grantor* or *Settlor* of the Trust. The trust document identifies who is to be the Trustee (caretaker) of property placed in the trust. Usually the Grantor appoints himself as Trustee so that he is in total control of property that he places into the trust. The trust document names a Successor Trustee who will take over the management of the trust property should the Trustee become disabled or die.

Once the trust document is properly signed, the Grantor transfers property into the trust. The Grantor does this by changing the name on the account from that of the Grantor to that of the Trustee. For example, if ELAINE RICHARDS sets up a trust naming herself as trustee, and she wishes to place her bank account into the trust then all she need do is instruct the bank to change the name on the account from ELAINE RICHARDS to:

ELAINE RICHARDS, TRUSTEE
of the ELAINE RICHARDS TRUST AGREEMENT dated 2/2/00

Once the change is made, all the money in the bank account becomes trust property. Elaine (wearing her trustee hat) still has total control of the account, taking money out and putting money in as she sees fit.

The trust document states how the trust property is to be managed during Elaine's lifetime. If the trust is a Revocable Lifetime Trust, then it will say that Elaine has the power to terminate the trust at any time and have all trust property returned to her. Should Elaine become disabled or die, then her Successor Trustee will take possession of the trust funds and manage (or distribute them) according the to direction Elaine gave in the trust document. If the trust says that once Elaine dies, the property is to be given to her beneficiary, then the Successor Trustee will do so; and in most cases without a probate procedure. If the trust directs the Successor Trustee to hold property in trust to care for a member of the Elaine's family, then the Successor Trustee will do so.

THE GOOD PART
Setting up a trust has many good features.

☆ AVOID GUARDIANSHIP PROCEDURES
If you become disabled or too aged to handle your finances, then you do not need to worry about who takes care of your finances. Your trust appoints a Successor Trustee to take over the care of your trust if you are unable to do so. If you do not have a trust and you become incapacitated, a court may need to appoint a guardian to take care for your property. The cost to establish and maintain the guardianship is charged to you. Guardianship procedures are expensive and once established cannot be terminated unless you die or are restored to health.

☆ AVOID PROBATE

You may be able to avoid probate by having your Successor Trustee distribute the trust property to your beneficiaries when you die. A trust is especially important if you own real property in more than one state. Without a trust, your Will may need to be probated in each state that you own property.

☆ CARE FOR A CHILD OR FAMILY MEMBER:

If you make provision in your trust to care for a child or a family member after you die, then your Successor Trustee can do so. If the family member is someone who is immature or a born spender, you can set up a Spendthrift Trust to protect the family member from squandering his inheritance. The Successor Trustee can see to it that the trust funds are used to pay for the family member's education or living expenses, and nothing more.

☆ TAX SAVINGS:

There can be substantial Estate tax savings if you are married and you and your spouse each set up your own trust. For example, suppose you and your spouse together have an estate worth one million dollars. You can each set up your own trust with $500,000. Each trust can provide that if one of you dies, the surviving spouse can use the income from the deceased partner's trust for living expenses. Once the second partner dies, all of the monies in the two trusts can be distributed, with no estate taxes due on either trust. By doing this, you each take advantage of your own Estate and Gift Tax Exclusion.

If you don't separate the funds, and one of you dies the surviving spouse has all of the money with only one deduction. Once the second dies, the entire amount is taxable. If the Exclusion amount is $675,000 and the Estate tax rate is 37%, then the beneficiaries will pay over $120,000 in Estate taxes.

☆ PRIVACY

Your trust is a private document. No one but your trustee and your beneficiaries need ever read it. If you leave property in a Will, and there is a probate procedure, the Will is filed with the Surrogate's court and becomes a public document.

THE PROBLEMS

For married people of means, it makes good sense to establish a trust. Others need to consider the downside:

⊠ COMPLEXITY

A trust is a fairly complex document, often 15 pages long. It needs to be that long because you are establishing a vehicle for taking care of your property during your lifetime, as well as after your death. The trust usually is written in "legalese," so it may take you considerable time and effort to understand it. It is important to work with an attorney who has the patience to work with you until you fully understand each paragraph of the document and are satisfied that this is what you want.

⊠ COST

Because of the complexity of the document and the fact that it is custom designed for you, a trust will cost much more to draft than a simple Will. In addition to the initial cost of the trust, it can be expensive to maintain the trust should you become disabled or die. Your Successor Trustee has the right to charge for his duties as trustee, as well as to charge for any specialized services performed. For example, if you choose an attorney to be Successor Trustee, then the attorney has the right to charge to manage the trust, and also charge for any legal work he performs. A financial institution can charge to serve as Successor Trustee, and also charge to manage the trust portfolio (Surrogate's 2307, 2309).

⊠ NO CREDITOR PROTECTION

Because property held in a Revocable Lifetime Trust is freely accessible to the Grantor, it is likewise accessible to his creditors both before and after the Grantor's death. If the Grantor dies owing money, then the trust funds can be used to pay for those debts (Estates 7-3.1(a)).

⊠ TAXES MAY STILL BE A PROBLEM:

While the Grantor is operating the trust as Trustee, all of the property held in a Revocable Living Trust is taxed as if the Grantor were holding that property in his/her own name. If the value of the trust property exceeds the Estate and Gift Tax Exclusion amount (see page 36 for the value), then unless the Grantor takes some other Estate Planning strategy, taxes will be due and owing once the Grantor dies.

⊠ PROBATE MIGHT STILL BE NECESSARY

The trust only works for those items that you place in the trust. If you have property that is held jointly with another, then when you die, that property will go to the joint owner and not to the trust. If you purchase a security in your name only, and forget to put it in your trust, there will need to be a probate procedure to determine the beneficiary of that security.

MAYBE PROBATE ISN'T ALL THAT BAD

As explained, if you hold all of your property in trust or jointly with another, you may be able to avoid probate and have your property go directly to your heirs. But you may have reason not to choose either of these methods. Perhaps you don't have money at this time to pay an attorney to set up a trust.

Perhaps you do not want to hold your money jointly with anyone because you are concerned about losing your independence or maybe you are concerned about keeping your money secure.

Still another reason for not holding property jointly is to be sure that your property is distributed in the way that you wish and according to the directions in your Will. If you want your money to go to several charities or to a minor child, then you may decide that it is better to make a Will rather than hold money jointly with just verbal instructions to your beneficiary about how you want the funds distributed when you die.

For example, if you hold all of your property jointly with your child, then the child is the legal owner of your property as of your date of death. If you tell your child to use some of that money for your grandchild's education, then that puts an unreasonable burden on your child because you were not specific as to exactly how much of that joint account was to be used for the child's education. Also you did not say how to use the money. Is the money for tuition only? Can the money be used to pay the child's living expenses?

Even if you give your child specific instructions about how the money is to be spent, and even if your child is honorable and with the best intentions, it may be that your grandchild gets none of the money, because your child is sued or falls upon hard times and is forced to use that money to pay debts. If you keep your property in your own name and leave a Will giving a certain amount of money for your grandchild, then he/she will know exactly how much money you left and the purpose of that gift.

If your grandchild is a minor at the time you make your Will you can appoint someone in your Will to be a custodian of the child's gift under The New York Uniform Transfers to Minors Act. The custodian can be a person or trust company or financial institution. The custodian is required by law to prudently care for the money or property until the child reaches the age of 21. The custodian may use as much of the money for the benefit of the minor as the custodian thinks advisable (Estates 7-6.14 and 7-6.20).

If you have a Will, and hold all of your money in your name only, then it will be distributed according to the directions you give in your Will. If there is a Summary or full Probate procedure the Surrogate's court will supervise the distribution. Any deviation from the instructions in your Will can be made only for good cause and with court approval.

PREPARING A WILL

Some people think they do not need to prepare a Will until they are very old and about to die. But according to reports published by the National Center for Health Statistics (a division of the U.S. Department of Health and Human Services) 2 of every 10 people who die in any given year are under the age of 60. Many will think that 20% is a small number until it hits close to home as it did with a young couple who were having difficulty conceiving a child. They went from doctor to doctor until they met someone just beginning his practice. With his knowledge of the latest advances in medicine, he was able to help them. The birth of their child was a moment of joy and gratitude. They asked a nurse to take a picture of them all together — the happy couple, the newborn child and the doctor who made it all happen. Happiness radiated from the picture, but one of them would be dead within six months.

You might think it was the child. An infant's life is so fragile. SIDS and all manner of childhood diseases can threaten a little one. But no, he grew up to be a healthy young man.

If you looked at the picture, you might guess the husband. Overweight, stressed out. His ruddy complexion suggested high blood pressure. He looked like he had a heart-attack-prone type A personality. But he was fine and went on to enjoy raising his son.

Probably the wife. She had such a difficult time with the pregnancy and the delivery was especially hard. Perhaps it was all too much for her. No, she recovered and later had two more children.

It was the doctor who was killed in a three car collision.

Though we all agree, that one never knows, still many procrastinate, rationalizing that if they die, New York law will take over and their property will be distributed in the manner that they would have wanted anyway. The problem with that reasoning is the complexity of the New York's Rules of Intestate Succession. If you are survived by a spouse, child, or parent, then it isn't too difficult to figure out who will inherit your property. But if none of these survive you, the ultimate beneficiary of your property may not be the person you would have chosen, had you taken the time to do so.

Others think that no Will is necessary because they have arranged their finances so that all of their property goes to their intended beneficiary automatically and without the need for probate. But it could happen that you die as a result of an accident, and someone will need to be appointed as your Personal Representative to sue on behalf of your estate. It is better to leave a Will so that you can say who will be in charge of handling your affairs once you die (your Personal Representative). If you don't have a Will and a probate procedure is necessary, then the Surrogate's court will choose someone for the job (see Page 27).

Still another benefit to making a Will is that you can make provision for who will get your personal property, including your car. Without a Will, your Personal Representative gets to make these decisions. With a Will you can make provision for the care of your child or grandchild. You can even provide for the care of your pet as these next few pages will show.

MAKE A GIFT OF YOUR CAR

As explained in Chapter 6, if you are married at the time of your death, then your spouse can transfer that car to his/her name.   All your spouse need do is to take the title to the car and a certified copy of the death certificate to the Department of Motor Vehicles.

If you do not have a surviving spouse or surviving child, then consider making a gift of your car in your Will. If you do so, then it will be relatively simple for your car to be transferred to the beneficiary (see Chapter 6 for how to transfer the car).

If you do not make a specific gift of your car in your Will, then it becomes part of your probate estate. Your Personal Representative can sell the car and include the proceeds of the sale in the estate funds to be distributed to your residuary beneficiaries.   If all you residuary beneficiaries agree, the Personal Representative can give the car to one of them as part of that beneficiary's share of the estate. If you die intestate, the car will go to your next of kin.

JOINT OWNERSHIP
Some may think it just as easy to hold the car jointly with the intended beneficiary — but the problem with joint ownership of a motor vehicle is liability.   If either owner is in an accident with the car, then both may be liable for any damage that is done.   If you are single, the better route is to hold title to the car in your name only and make a gift of the car in your Will.

FOR PET LOVERS

A woman died at peace,
leaving her fortune
and care of her cat to her niece.
Alas, the fortune and the cat
Soon disappeared after that.

You could leave your money to someone and ask they use part of it to care for your pet, but the moral of the above limerick, is that leaving your money to someone to do the job may not be the best route to go.

 **TRUST FOR CARE OF PET**

If you are serious about caring for your pet after your death, you can employ an attorney to set up a separate trust for the care of your pet, or you can have the attorney include a trust provision in your Will. New York law provides that such a trust is valid and will be honored up until the pet dies, or 21 years have passed.

You can appoint someone to be trustee of the funds and to use the monies for the care of the pet. You also need to name a beneficiary (a person or charitable organization) to receive whatever may remain in the trust once the pet dies. If you do not name anyone, then the remainder will go to whoever inherited your estate (Estates 7-6.1).

You can ask the trustee to be custodian of the pet. If so, you can ask the beneficiary to regularly check on the pet and to see to it that the pet is treated humanely, if not benevolently.

CARE OF PETS (Continued)

If you don't have the resources to set up a trust to care for your pet, you can still ask a fellow pet lover to care for the animal. If no one among your circle of family and friends is able to do so, then ask your pet's veterinarian to consider starting an "Orphaned Pet Service" to assist in finding new homes for pets who lose their owners. It is good public relations and a potential source of income. People can make provision in their Will to pay the Veterinarian to care for the pet until a suitable family can be found. That is a more humane approach than the, all to common practice, of putting a pet "to sleep" rather than have the pet suffer the loss of its master. And in at least one case, that reasoning backfired.

Eleanor always had a pet in the house. After her husband died, her two poodles were her constant companions. When Eleanor became ill with cancer, she worried about what would happen to her "buddies" if she died. She finally decided it best to have her family put them to sleep when she died.

Eleanor endured surgery, chemotherapy, radiation therapy, and even some holistic remedies, but she continued to go downhill. Eleanor's family came in to visit her at the hospital to say their last good-byes. She was so ill, she didn't even recognize them. No one thought she could last the day. Because the family was from out of state, and time short, they decided to put the pets to sleep so they need only take care of the funeral arrangements when she died. To everyone's surprise, Eleanor rallied. She lived two more long, lonely years.

She often said she wished they had put her to sleep instead of her buddies.

PROVIDING FOR THE CHILD

Parents have a special responsibility. They need to make provision for the care of their child in the event they both die or become incapacitated before the child is grown. It is unusual for a child to lose both parents, but it does happen, and parents need to provide for this eventuality.

CARING FOR THE PERSON OF THE CHILD

A child must be cared for in two ways, the *person* of the child and *property* of the child. To care for the person of the child, someone must be in charge of the child's everyday living, not only food and shelter but to provide social, ethical and religious training. Someone must have legal authority to make medical decisions and see to the child's education.

To care for the property of the child, someone must take charge of monies left to the child. That person is responsible to see that the monies are used for the care of the child and that anything left over is preserved until the child becomes an adult. If one parent becomes incapacitated or dies, then the other parent has the right (and duty) to be the guardian of their minor child.

New York statute gives each parent the right to appoint a guardian to care for the person and property of their minor child in the event that they both are incapacitated or deceased. The parent can appoint a guardian of the child's person and a guardian of the child's property, or one person to be guardian of the child's person and property.

Each parent can appoint a guardian as part of his or her Will. For the appointment to be effective, the other parent must agree to the appointment by signing a sworn written statement stating that the consenting parent:

- ☑ agrees to the choice of guardian;
- ☑ is motivated solely by the welfare of the child;
- ☑ has not and will not receive any consideration for such consent;
- ☑ understands that he/she can revoke this consent at any time prior to the death of the other parent by filing the revocation in the office of the county clerk where the other parent lives.

It is best if both parents choose the same person to serve as guardian for their child, however, they can choose different people. If they choose different guardians and both parents die simultaneously, then the Surrogate's court will decide which of the guardians should be appointed (Domestic Relations 81).

LEAVING PROPERTY FOR THE CHILD

As any parent is well aware, it is expensive to raise a child. People that you might consider to be the best choice to serve as your child's guardian might not be able to do so unless you leave sufficient monies to pay for the care of the child. If you are a person of limited finances, then consider purchasing a term life insurance policy on your life and/or on the life of the other parent of the child. If you can only afford one policy, then insure the life of the parent who contributes most to the support of the child.

Term insurance policies are relatively inexpensive if you limit the term to just that period of time until your child becomes an adult. Some companies offer a combination of term life and disability insurance. As with any other purchase, it is important to comparison shop to obtain the best price for the coverage.

FOR PARENTS OF A MINOR CHILD (continued)

If you are married to the parent of your child, then the beneficiary of the term insurance policy can be your spouse with your child as an alternate beneficiary. Married or single, you can name your child as the primary beneficiary of the policy. If you name the child as beneficiary of a policy that is $10,000 or less, and you die before the child turns 18, then the insurance funds will be given to the child's other parent, to be used for the benefit of the child.

If the amount exceeds $10,000, then a guardian of the property, will need to be appointed to take custody of the insurance proceeds. In such case, the judge usually appoints the surviving parent as the guardian of child's property. The court will not allow the guardian of the child's property, to spend any of the insurance funds without court approval. The court will require that the guardian give the court an annual accounting to be sure that the monies are being preserved for the benefit of the child. Once the child turns 18, the court will supervise the distribution of the monies to the child.

The child's monies are protected but the downside is the cost of setting up a guardianship. There are filing fees and attorney fees and perhaps monies will need to be spent to pay an accountant to give the court a formal accounting. As explained on page 164, the better route is to name someone as serve as custodian of the insurance funds under the NEW YORK UNIFORM TRANSFERS TO MINORS ACT.

 **LAWYER** | PREPARE A TRUST FOR THE CHILD

If you have sufficient monies to care for your child until adulthood, then consult with an attorney about setting up a trust for the child or drafting a Will with a trust provision in the event you die before the child is grown. You will need to appoint a trustee to handle the trust funds as the child is growing. You can appoint the other parent of the child as the trustee. You will need to appoint a successor trustee in the event that the other parent is unable to serve as trustee.

You can appoint the same person to serve as trustee as you have chosen to serve as Guardian of the person of the child, but it may be better to appoint two different people for these jobs. The desirable qualities of a guardian are essentially those of a "people person" someone who is sensitive to the child's emotional needs — someone who will love and nurture the child.

The important qualities of a trustee are honesty, trustworthiness and being knowledgeable in money matters. The trustee will be in charge of giving sufficient money to the guardian for the child's maintenance. Consider choosing a trustee who is not overly generous so that all of the funds will be spent before the child is grown, yet not so thrifty that the child has little quality of life in his formative years.

If you are successful in your choice, the child will be fortunate to have two such adults to guide him through his childhood.

PROVIDING FOR THE STEPCHILD

Perhaps the reason that the story of Cinderella has such universal appeal, is that many stepchildren, at one point or another, feel left out. Even the law seems to reinforce that perception. For example, if you have a stepchild, then that child has no intestate rights to your estate. If you and your spouse (the child's natural parent) hold all property jointly, and your spouse dies first, then your stepchild will be left nothing unless you make some provision for the child in your Will.

Should your spouse die, then you, and not your stepchild, have the authority to agree to an autopsy or an anatomical gift. Even during your spouse's lifetime, you, and not your stepchild, have the authority to make a Do-Not-Resuscitate decision in the event that your spouse is too ill to make medical decisions.

Of course, giving you authority to make medical decisions and giving you the right to inherit all of your spouse's estate must be something that is agreeable to the child's natural parent. If your spouse wants the child to have primary authority to make medical decisions, then your spouse can sign a Health Care Proxy appointing the child (and not you) as Health Care Agent (see page 156). Similarly, if your spouse wants his/her child to inherit property, then your spouse can arrange his/her finances so that the child will inherit property. Hopefully, your spouse will consult with an estate planning attorney who can explain the best way to achieve that goal, else that intent could be thwarted and the child end up with little or nothing, as was the case in the example given on page 111.

PROVIDING FOR THE ADULT CHILD

It isn't just step-children who can be left out if no provision is made. Even children from a long-standing marriage can be cut off against the wishes of a parent. A parent may assume that all of their children will be treated equally once they are both gone, but consider that the last to die is the one who gets to decide "who gets what." That was the case with Joan and Herbert. They were a devoted couple, married over forty years. Herb was the bread-winner, but he was content to let Joan handle all of the finances.

Joan wanted to be sure that each of their three daughters would always have a decent place to live. They purchased a three story house and each of the daughters moved into a different floor of the home. It was the parent's intent that once they were both gone, the daughters would inherit and occupy the building.

The couple held everything jointly. When Joan died, all of their property, including the home, was owned by Herbert. The grief suffered by Herbert at his wife's passing was more than he could bear. He alternated between sadness, anger and despair. He seemed to take out his anger on his middle daughter. Their relationship had always been strained. She felt she could never live up to her father's expectations. She was not the cute baby of the family as was her younger sister. She was not the eldest daughter who always seemed to make her Dad proud. He always made her feel that she was a disappointment to him. Once her mother died, she had no one left to buffer the relationship with her father.

Within three months of Joan's death, Herbert had an attorney draft a Will leaving all to his eldest and youngest daughter. None of the children knew what he had done.

Herbert decided to take a trip to Europe to try to escape the pain of his mourning. When he was in France, he suffered a massive heart attack and died. It was less than 6 months from the time of Joan's death.

Had he returned from Europe, he may have reconciled with his daughter, but as it happened, there was no time for them to develop a better relationship.

With both their parents gone, the eldest and youngest daughter decided to sell the home. The youngest sister offered some of the proceeds to middle daughter. The middle daughter responded with anger. Being offered less than her one-third share, meant to her, that her sisters approved of their father's action. It was as if she were being disinherited all over again.

It was unfortunate that Joan's best plans were thwarted. They didn't have to be. She and Herbert could have kept a life estate in the property with the remainder going to all three girls. That would have ensured that each daughter received an equal inheritance. More importantly, the family would not have been torn by the hurt and anger that was more a product of a husband's grief rather than the absence of a father's love.

 **LAWYER**

PROVIDE FOR
THE INCAPACITATED

If you are the caretaker or legal guardian of someone who is incapacitated, then in addition to preparing your own estate plan, you need to be concerned about what will happen to the incapacitated person should you die. Someone will need to make medical decisions for the incapacitated person and see to it that he/she is properly housed and fed.

APPOINTMENT OF A SUCCESSOR CARETAKER

Often a family member will agree to take responsibility for the care of an incapacitated person in the event that the caretaker dies. But perhaps no one wants the job, or the opposite case, too many want to have control. For example, if a parent is incapacitated, one child may want the parent to remain at home with the assistance of a home health care worker. Another child may think the best place for the parent is an assisted living facility with 24 hour care. The caretaker spouse may be concerned that a tug-of-war will erupt once he dies.

In such cases, the caretaker should consult with an attorney to ensure future care for the incapacitated person. The attorney may suggest establishing a trust or having a legal guardian appointed for the incapacitated person while the parent/caretaker is alive. Once the guardianship is in place, the court will continue to supervise the care of the incapacitated person until he/she dies.

 **LAWYER**

A SPECIAL NEEDS TRUST FOR THE INCAPACITATED

If a person is incapacitated, both the federal and state government provide assistance with programs such as social security disability benefits and custodial nursing home care under the Medicaid program. The family often supplements the government program by providing for the incapacitated person's *special needs*, such as clothing, hobbies, special education, outings to a movie or special event — things that give the incapacitated person some quality of life.

To be eligible for government assistance programs the incapacitated must be essentially without funds. Caretakers fear that leaving money to the incapacitated in a will or trust will disqualify the incapacitated from further government assistance. Understanding this dilemma, both the federal and New York state government allow caretakers to set up a trust that supplements government benefits. New York statute (Estates 7-1.12) authorizes setting up a *Supplemental Needs Trust.* If the trust is set up with the incapacitated person's assets, then a *Disability Trust* as authorized by the Federal government (42 U.S.C. 1382c(a)(3)) can be established. A trustee is appointed to use trust funds to provide for the special needs of the incapacitated. If any trust funds are left after the incapacitated dies, then those funds must be used to reimburse the state for monies spent on behalf of the incapacitated person.

There are other types of special needs trusts that are allowed under the law. An experienced Elder Law attorney can explain the different options available and assist the family member in preparing a Will or trust that will provide for the incapacitated person's special needs once the family member dies.

PROVIDING FOR YOUR OWN INCAPACITY

As the life expectancy of the population increases, so does the percentage of the population who suffer a stroke or other type of debilitating diseases such as Alzheimer's, or Parkinsons'. It is estimated that more than 50% of the population who are 85 or older, suffer some degree of dementia as a result of these degenerative diseases. If you are concerned that you may become disabled in the future, you need to consider who will care for your property and who will take care of your person.

CARING FOR YOUR PROPERTY: If you have significant assets, you can have an attorney prepare a trust. You can be trustee of the funds while you have capacity. Once you can no longer do so, then the person you name as Successor Trustee will take over. If you do not have sufficient assets to justify the cost of a trust, then consider having your attorney draft a Durable Power of Attorney. This document gives the person of your choice (your *Agent*) authority to care for your finances in the event of your incapacity. You can discuss with your attorney those things that you do (or do not) wish your Agent to do on your behalf. Your attorney can prepare a Power of Attorney especially designed to meet your needs.

New York statute (General Obligations 5-1501) provides a short form of the Durable Power of Attorney. If you wish you can use the statutory form to appoint your Agent. To do so you need to complete the form properly and sign it in the presence of two witnesses and a notary public.

CARING FOR YOUR PERSON: You can have your attorney prepare a Health Care Proxy to appoint a Health Care Agent to make your medical decisions should you become incapacitated. As discussed on page 156 there is a statutory form that you can use if you wish to prepare your own Proxy.

 **LAWYER**

WILL IS NOT BEST VEHICLE FOR LARGE ESTATES

A simple Will is not the best route to go if you have a large estate. The cost of probate is significant for large estates. Your Personal Representative is entitled to reasonable compensation which, according to New York statute (Surrogate's 2307) is as follows:

> 5% for estates of $100,000 or less
> 4% of the next $200,000
> 3% of the next $700,000
> 2 1/2% of the next 4 million dollars
> 2% of all sums over 5 million dollars

This works out to be $34,000 for the first million dollars. Attorney's fees could well cost an additional $34,000, so an estate of one million dollars could cost your beneficiaries $68,000 for just attorney and Personal Representative fees. In addition, there will be court costs, accounting fees, appraisal fees, and probably Estate taxes. A good chunk of your estate can be "eaten up" by these fees and costs.

Also, consider that people with large estates have the ability to run up debts large enough to demolish any hope of passing anything onto their heirs. An experienced estate planning attorney can advise a wealthy person how to protect his assets, both before and after death.

If you have an estate that is large enough to incur Estate taxes (see page 36 for the table of values), then it is important to consult with an attorney to avoid probate; to reduce, if not eliminate, Estate taxes; and to preserve your estate assets for the next generation.

 **LAWYER**   BUSINESS OWNER

One type of estate that is most difficult to settle is that of a person who owns (and manages) a business and who suddenly dies. It is difficult enough to settle an estate when all the decedent left was a home and some personal property. If the decedent left an ongoing business, and he was the only one in charge, then that really complicates matters, especially if there are employees who depend on the business for their livelihood.

If you are a business owner, and you do some thinking and planning, you can save your family (and employees) time, effort and probably money. In particular, you need to be concerned about two things: the orderly transfer of the business and the payment of business debts. An attorney who is experienced in business law (corporation, banking, bankruptcy, franchise law, etc.) can offer suggestions as to the best method of ensuring that the business continues its operation, or terminates in an orderly fashion — whichever is applicable in your case. Discuss how company debts will be paid and how best to distribute the company assets to your heirs, in case of your death.

Let your accountant know who is to have access to your business records in the event of your incapacity or death. If it is your intent that the business continue in your absence, you might consider purchasing key man insurance on your life to compensate the company for any loss suffered because of your absence. See page 43 for an explanation of key man insurance.

ARRANGING TO PAY BILLS

When people draft a Will they are more concerned about giving their possessions away than they are about taking into account what they actually have to give. This was the case with Larry. He had no family to speak of. After his wife died, he bought a condominium in retirement community. Over the years, he developed a close network of friends. They became his family. Larry did not have much money. His car was leased. He had a mortgage on the condominium. He wanted his friends to know how much they meant to him so he had a Will drafted giving all he owned to five close friends.

The friends appreciated the gesture but the probate procedure turned out to be a nightmare. They had to keep current the mortgage payments and the maintenance fees until the condominium was sold. Because Larry left little cash, this money had to come out of the beneficiaries' pockets. Two were living on their social security income and they had to borrow money from the others to contribute to their share of the upkeep.

The beneficiaries had no money to settle the lease on the car. Even if they did, they decided that there was no point in doing so because the amount needed to obtain clear title was greater than the current market value of the car. The beneficiaries decided not to make any further payment and they returned the car to the leasing agent. Their decision turned out to be a losing proposition. The leasing agent took the car, sold it and then sued the estate for the balance of the monies owed on the lease.

Because the beneficiaries had to quickly liquidate the estate, the condominium sold for less than it would have had they the time, energy and resources to fix it up. After they settled with the leasing agent, paid off the funeral expenses, mortgage, and probate fees there was only a few hundred dollars left. That was a lot of work and stress for nothing.

The pity was that Larry could have arranged his finances so that his beneficiaries were not burdened by his debt. He could have taken out mortgage insurance as part of the loan package. In most cases the cost of the insurance is nominal and is included as part of the monthly mortgage payment.

Larry could have done the same when he leased the car. Most leasing contracts offer term life insurance as an option. The cost of such insurance depends on the age of the person, the term of the loan and the amount of monies owed, but the premium paid each month is just a small fraction of the loan payment.

Even if Larry just arranged for payment of one of these debts, his beneficiaries would have come away with the gift that Larry intended, instead of the headache that they inherited.

PROVIDE FOR CREDIT CARD DEBT

If you have significant credit card debt, you need to consider how that debt will be paid once you die. Most credit card companies offer insurance policies and include the premium as part of your monthly payment. If you have such insurance, then should you die, any outstanding balance is paid. It benefits the credit card company to offer life insurance as part of the credit package, because they are assured of prompt payment should the borrower die. However, if you have little or no assets and no one other than yourself is liable to pay the debt, you may have no incentive to pay for insurance that can only benefit the lender.

As discussed in Chapters 2 and 4, if you hold a credit card jointly with another person, both of you are equally liable to pay the debt. If one of you dies, the other is responsible to pay the bill regardless of who ran up the bill. If paying that bill could be a struggle for the surviving debtor, then the better route to go is for each of you to have your own credit card.

Still another reason not to hold a joint credit card is that each of you can establish your own line of credit. This is especially important if you are married and one of you is retired or has been out of the job market for any period of time. Should the breadwinner die, it may be difficult for the surviving partner to establish credit if he/she has no recent work record It is easier for the unemployed spouse to establish a line of credit when he/she is married to someone who is working.

PURCHASE LIFE INSURANCE

The good part of purchasing loan insurance — be it credit card insurance, mortgage insurance or car insurance, is that you can usually purchase the insurance without taking a medical examination. The down side, is that such insurance may be more expensive than a life insurance policy. If you are in fairly good health, consider taking out a life insurance policy to cover all of your outstanding loans. The cost of the single life insurance policy may be significantly less than purchasing separate loan insurance policies. This strategy works best if you are married and your spouse is jointly liable for the mortgage and car payment. If you name your spouse as beneficiary, then he/she can use the funds to pay off all of your joint debts.

If you name someone as beneficiary who has no legal obligation to pay your debts and if your primary residence is in the state of New York, none of your creditors can force your beneficiary to use any part of those funds to pay your debts (Insurance 3212 (b)). If you want the insurance funds used to pay your debts, then this may not be the way to go. But, if you want to be sure that someone receives money for their care after you are gone, and you do not want those funds reduced by the cost of probate or to pay off your debts, then this strategy should accomplish your goal.

Which brings us to the issue of life insurance — should you have it? How much is enough? The answer to these questions depends on the "sleep at night" factor, namely how much insurance do you need to make you not worry about insurance coverage when you go to sleep at night? It is often more an emotional than a financial issue.

Some people have an "every man for himself" attitude and are content to have no life insurance at all. Others worry about how their loved ones will manage if they are not around to support them. The same person may have different thoughts about insurance coverage as the circumstances of their life changes — from no coverage in their bachelor days to more-than-enough coverage in their child rearing days to just-enough-to-bury-me in their senior years. Insurance companies recognize that people's needs change over the years. Many companies offer flexible insurance coverage. As with any consumer item, it is a good idea to shop around.

In addition to life insurance, you might want to consider long-term health care insurance. Your best estate plan could be sabotaged by a lengthy, or debilitating illness. If you are poor, long-term nursing care may not be of concern to you, because all your needs should be covered under Medicaid. If you are very wealthy, you may not worry because you have more than enough money to pay for your care. But the rest of us need to think about ways to provide for long-term health care. An experienced Elder law attorney can suggest an estate plan that will preserve your assets in the event of a lengthy illness.

If long-term care insurance is part of your estate plan, then you need to consider the many plans that are available. You can get the publication A SHOPPER'S GUIDE TO LONG-TERM CARE INSURANCE, free of charge from the National Association of Insurance Commissioners by calling (816) 460-7593. If you have specific questions about long-term care insurance then you can call the New York State Office for the Aging at (800) 333-4114. The State Office for the Aging Department also has information at their Web site:

 NEW YORK STATE OFFICE FOR THE AGING
http://www.aging.state.ny.us/

ANNUITIES TO SPREAD INSURANCE BENEFITS

Most beneficiaries go through their inheritance within two years. For many, the reason the money is gone so soon, is that there just wasn't much money to inherit in the first place. But for others, it's a spending frenzy.

People's spending habits remain much the same throughout their lifetime. Some people are squirrels, always saving for the winter. For others, it's:

Earn-A-Penny   Spend-A-Penny

Most of us fall somewhere in between. We are not extravagant in our spending habits, yet it is a struggle to save. But why should we struggle to purchase an insurance policy if the intended beneficiary will spend it in a few months?

If you want to leave an insurance policy benefit to someone you love, but the intended beneficiary is immature, or a born spendthrift, then a simple solution to the problem may be to purchase an annuity rather than life insurance. The annuity can be set up so that the beneficiary receives money on a monthly, or yearly basis, rather than a single lump sum payment when you die. There are many different types of annuities, so again, it is important to shop around.

CHOOSING THE RIGHT ESTATE PLAN

Joint Ownership?
A Life Estate?
An "in trust for" bank account?
A Will?
A Revocable Lifetime Trust?
An Insurance Policy???

This chapter offers so many options that the reader may be more confused than when he was blissfully unenlightened.

As with most things in life, you may find there are no ultimate solutions, just alternatives. The right choice for you is the one that best accomplishes your goal. This being the case, you first need to determine what you want to accomplish with the money you leave behind. Think about what will happen to your property if you were to die suddenly, without making any plan different from the one you now have.
Who will get your property?
Will there be any estate tax?
Will they need to go through a full probate procedure?

If the answers to these questions are not what you wish, then you need to work to retitle your property to accomplish your goals. For those with significant assets, — especially those with estates large enough to pay estate taxes, a trip to an experienced Estate Planning attorney may be well worth the consultation fee.

Once you are satisfied with your estate plan, then the final thing to determine is whether your heirs will be able to locate your assets once you are deceased.

Most people have their business records in one place, their Will in another place, car titles and deeds in still another place. When someone dies, their beneficiaries may feel as if they are playing a game of "hide and seek" with the decedent. The game might be fun if it were not for the fact that things not found may be forever lost. For example, suppose you die in an accident and no one knows you are insured by your credit card company for accidental death in the amount of $50,000. The only one to profit is the insurance company, which is just that much richer because no one told them that you died as a result of an accident.

How about a key to a safe deposit box located in another state? Will anyone find it? Even if they find the key, how will they find the box?

It is not difficult to arrange things so that your affairs are always in order. It amounts to being aware of what you own (and owe) and keeping a record of your possessions. A side benefit is that by doing so, you will always know where all your business records are. If you ever spent time trying to collect information to file your taxes or trying to find a lost stock or bond certificate, you will appreciate the value of organizing your records.

THE *If I Die* FILE

Your heirs will have no problem locating your assets if you keep all of your records a single place. It can be a desk drawer or a file cabinet or even a shoe box. If you wish to keep all of your original documents in a safe deposit box, then make a copy of each document and keep the copy in your home with a note saying where the original can be found. It is helpful if you keep a separate file or folder for each type of investment. You might consider setting up the following folders:

 ## THE BANK & SECURITIES FOLDER

The BANK & SECURITIES FOLDER is for original certificates of deposit, stock, bonds or mutual funds. The folder should contain a copy of the contract you signed with each financial institution. The contract will show where you have funds and who you named as beneficiary or joint owner of the account. If someone owes you money and has signed a Promissory note or mortgage that identifies you as the lender, then you can store such documents in this folder as well.

If you have a safe deposit box, then keep a record of the location of the box and box number in this folder. Make a copy of all of the items in the box (including jewelry), and place the copies in a folder entitled CONTENTS OF SAFE DEPOSIT BOX. You may wish to attach an envelope to the folder and put your safe deposit key in that envelope. It will probably take a court order to remove items from the box once you die and it will be helpful if your heirs know exactly what is in the safe deposit box.

📁 THE DEED FOLDER

Many people save every scrap of paper associated with the closing of real property. If you closed recently on real estate and there was a mortgage involved in the purchase, you probably walked away from closing with enough paper to wallpaper your kitchen. If you wish, you can keep all of those papers in a separate file that identifies the property, for example:

CLOSING PAPERS FOR THE ALBANY CONDO

Set aside the original deed (or a copy if the original is in a safe deposit box) and place it into a separate DEED FOLDER. Include deeds to parcels of real property, cemetery deeds, condominium deeds, cooperative shares to real property, time-sharing certificates, etc. Include deeds to out of state property as well as New York property in the DEED FOLDER. If you have a mortgage on your property, then put a copy of the mortgage and promissory note in a separate LIABILITY FOLDER.

📁 THE INSURANCE/PENSION FOLDER

The INSURANCE FOLDER is for each original insurance policy that you own, be it car insurance, homeowner's insurance or a health care insurance policy. If you purchased real property, you probably received a title commitment at closing and the original title insurance policy some weeks later when you received your original deed from recording. If you cannot locate the title insurance policy, then contact the closing agent and have them send you a copy of your title policy. If you have a pension or an annuity, then include those documents in this folder as well.

🗁 THE PERSONAL PROPERTY FOLDER

MOTOR VEHICLES
Put all motor vehicle titles in Personal Property folder. This includes cars, mobile homes, boats, planes, etc. If you owe money on the vehicle, the lender may have possession of the title certificate. If such is the case, then put a copy of the registration in this folder and a copy of the promissory note or chattel mortgage in a separate liability folder.

If you have a boat or plane, then identify the location of the motor vehicle. For example, if you are leasing space in an airplane hanger or in a marina, then keep a copy of the leasing agreement in this file.

JEWELRY
If you own expensive jewelry, then keep a picture of the item together with the sales receipt or written appraisal in this folder.

COLLECTOR'S ITEMS
If you own a valuable art collection, or a coin collection or any other item of significant value, then include a picture of the item in this file. Also include evidence of ownership of the item, such as a sales receipt or a certificate of authenticity, or a written appraisal of the personal property.

📁 THE LIABILITY FOLDER

The LIABILITY FOLDER should contain all loan documents of debts that you owe. For example, if you purchased real property and have a mortgage on that property, then put a copy of the mortgage and promissory note in this folder. If you owe money on a car, then put the promissory note and chattel mortgage on the car in the file. If you have a credit card, then put a copy of the contract you signed with the credit card company in this file.

Many people never take the time to calculate their *net worth* (what a person owns less what that person owes). By having a record of your outstanding debts, you can calculate your net worth whenever you wish.

📁 THE TAX RECORD FOLDER

Your Personal Representative (or next of kin) will need to file your final income tax return. Keep a copy of your tax returns (both federal and state) for the past three years in your Tax Record Folder.

🗂 THE PERSONAL RECORD FOLDER

The PERSONAL RECORD FOLDER should include documents that relate to you personally, such as a birth certificate, naturalization papers, pre-nuptial or post- nuptial agreement, Will or Trust, marriage certificate, divorce papers, army records, social security card; etc. If you have a Health Care Proxy or a Power of Attorney, then this is a good place to keep those documents.

FOR FEDERAL RETIREES
If you are a Federal Retiree, then you should have received your **PERSONAL IDENTIFICATION NUMBER (PIN)** and your survivor annuitant should have received his/her own PIN as well. It is relatively simple to obtain this during your lifetime, but it may be difficult and/or stressful for your survivor annuitant to work through the system once you are gone. To get information on obtaining these numbers you can call the RETIREMENT INFORMATION OFFICE at 1-888-767-6738. For the hard of hearing, call 1-800-878-5707.

Upon your death, your family may be entitled to death benefits. These benefits are not automatic. Your family member (your "survivor") must apply for them by submitting a death claim to the Office of Personnel Management. Your survivor needs to know that it is necessary to apply and also how to apply. See page 30 for an explanation about how to apply for benefits and then make that information available to your family. You can either put this information in the insurance/pension folder or in your Personal Record folder.

THE *If I Die* FILE

In addition to keeping your records in a single place, you need to let your family know the location of these items. You can set up an *If I Die* file and give that file to your next of kin or the person you appointed as Personal Representative in your Will.

You can use the form on the next page as a basis for the information to include in the file.

If I Die

then the following information will help settle my estate:

INFORMATION FOR DEATH CERTIFICATE

MY FULL LEGAL NAME _____

MY SOCIAL SECURITY NO. _____

MY USUAL OCCUPATION _____

BIRTH DATE AND BIRTH PLACE _____

If naturalized, date & place _____

MY FATHER'S NAME _____

MY MOTHER'S MAIDEN NAME _____

PERSONS TO BE NOTIFIED OF MY DEATH

_____

_____

_____

FUNERAL AND BURIAL ARRANGEMENTS

LOCATION OF BURIAL SITE

_____

LOCATION OF PRENEED FUNERAL CONTRACT

_____

FOR VETERAN or SPOUSE BURIAL IN A NATIONAL CEMETERY

BRANCH_____SERIAL NO._____

VETERAN'S RANK _____

VETERAN'S VA CLAIM NUMBER _____

DATE AND PLACE OF ENTRY INTO SERVICE:

_____

DATE AND PLACE OF SEPARATION FROM SERVICE:

_____

LOCATION OF OFFICIAL MILITARY DISCHARGE
   OR DD 214 FORM_____

LOCATION OF LEGAL DOCUMENTS

BIRTH CERTIFICATE _____

MARRIAGE CERTIFICATE_____

DIVORCE DECREE _____

PASSPORT _____

WILL OR TRUST _____

DEEDS _____

MORTGAGES _____

TITLE TO MOTOR VEHICLES _____

HEALTH CARE DIRECTIVES _____

NAME, PHONE NO. OF ATTORNEY_____

LOCATION OF FINANCIAL RECORDS

INSURANCE POLICIES:

NAME OF COMPANY & PHONE NO. _____

LOCATION OF POLICY _____

BENEFICIARY OF POLICY _____

PENSIONS/ANNUITIES:

IF FEDERAL RETIREE: PIN NUMBER: _____

NAME OF SURVIVOR _____

SURVIVOR PIN NUMBER _____

BANK

BANK: ACCOUNT NO._____

NAME, ADDRESS OF FINANCIAL INSTITUTION

_____

LOCATION OF SAFE DEPOSIT BOX _____

LOCATION OF KEY TO BOX _____

SECURITIES

NAME AND PHONE NUMBER OF BROKER

_____

TAX RECORDS FOR PAST 3 YEARS

LOCATION _____

ACCOUNTANT: NAME, PHONE # _____

_____

GAMES DECEDENTS PLAY

We discussed the game of "hide and seek" some decedents play with their heirs. A variation of that game is the "wild goose chase." The decedent never updates his files, so his records are filled with all sorts of lapsed insurance policies, promissory notes of debts long since paid; brokerage statements of securities that have been sold. The family spend much wasted time trying to locate the "missing" asset.

The best joke is to keep the key to a safe deposit box that you are no longer leasing. That will keep folks hunting for a long time!

If you do not have a wicked sense of humor, then do your family a favor and update your records on a regular basis.

WHEN TO UPDATE YOUR ESTATE PLAN

We discussed people's natural disinclination to make an estate plan until they are faced with their own mortality. Many believe that they will make just one Will and then die (maybe that's why they put off making a Will). The reality is, that most people who make a Will, change it at least once before they die.

If you have an estate plan, it is important to update it when any of the following things take place:

RELOCATION TO A NEW STATE OR COUNTRY
Each state (and country) has its own laws relating to the inheritance of property and those laws are very different from each other. Items that are protected from a creditor in one state, may not be creditor proof in another state. Each state has its own estate tax structure. If estate taxes are high, you may need an estate plan that will minimize the impact of those taxes.

Each state has its own, unique, laws of intestate succession. Who has the right to inherit your property in one state may be very different from who can inherit your property in another. The rights of a spouse in a community property state are very different from those in other states. Even if you have a Will, what one state considers to be a valid Will, may be different from what another state considers to be valid.

If you move to another state or country, then it is important to either educate yourself about the laws of the state, or to consult with an attorney who can assist you in reviewing your estate plan to see if that plan will accomplish your goals in that state.

A SIGNIFICANT CHANGE IN THE LAW
It is important to keep up with changes in the law. You can do so by just reading your daily newspaper. Happily, laws relating to the inheritance of property and the way estates are probated, have remained stable over the years. Tax laws however, are in a constant state of flux. You need to be aware of how the tax structure is being changed and how that change affects your estate plan. Often times, the change in the law is so complicated, that you will need the assistance of your accountant or attorney to explain how the new law impacts your estate plan.

A CHANGE IN RELATIONSHIP
If you get married, divorced, have a child, lose a beneficiary of your estate, then you should examine your estate plan to determine whether it needs to be revised.

There are statutory provisions that change certain of your estate planning documents in the event of a divorce, for example, if you get divorced and neglect to change your Will, and then die in New York, the Surrogate's court will read your Will as if your spouse died just before you did (Estates 5-1.3). Also, if you appointed your spouse as your Health Care Agent, and later divorce, then that appointment is revoked by New York law (Public Health 2985 (e)).

Although the statute eliminates your spouse, it does not appoint another in his/her place. For example, if you appointed your spouse as your Executor of your Will, then you need to appoint someone else to do the job. Similarly, if you appointed your spouse as your Health Care Agent, then you need to appoint someone else. It is best not to rely on New York statute, but rather to revoke the document yourself and revise your estate plan to fit your changed circumstances.

Completing The Process 9

The funeral is over.

Everyone went home.

You experienced and got past the initial grief.

All the affairs of the decedent have been settled.

You even did some of the things suggested in Chapters 7 and 8 so you feel that your own affairs are now in order. But is the grieving over? Do you have closure? To use a tired expression, have you been able to "get on with your life" or do you find that you are still grieving?

And how about the children in the decedent's life? How are they taking the loss?

The death event is not over until the family finally finds peace and acceptance of the loss. This chapter deals with issues that may arise as the family goes through the grieving process.

THE GRIEVING PROCESS

Psychologists have observed that it is common for a person to go through a series of stages as part of the grieving process. There is the initial shock of the death and often disbelief and denial:

"He can't be dead. I just spoke to him today!"

It is common for a mourner to be angry — angry at the decedent for dying — angry at a family member for something he should or shouldn't have done — just plain angry.

Sometimes an ill person is aware of his impending death and becomes angry, as if mourning his own death. Relations with the family may become strained under the stress of the illness. If there was an argument with the decedent, the bereaved may be left with an unresolved conflict and feelings of guilt.

Mourners often experience guilt. Many have an uneasy feeling that the death was somehow their fault. Some regret not having spent more time with the decedent. Others feel guilty because they weren't present when the decedent died.

There is grieving even when death is long expected and even welcomed. This was the case with a wife who nursed her husband at home for nine long years. Her husband suffered from debilitating strokes, a chronic heart condition, and finally failing kidneys. She often said "Some things are worse than death." Yet when he died, she was surprised at the depth of her emotions.

Although professionals in the fields of psychiatry and psychology have observed that guilt and anger are stages of grieving, there is no agreement about the number or composition of the stages of grieving.

This not surprising. The ways people react to death is as diverse as there are people. Some people seem not to grieve at all. Whether such people experience any stage of the grieving process may not be known even to the person himself/herself.

And there is diversity in grieving even in the same person. Each circumstance of death in one's life is different from another, so a person will grieve differently when different people in their life die. But for purposes of this discussion, we note that many people who lose someone they love, report experiencing the following emotions and in the following sequence:

- initial shock, disbelief, alarm
- numbness, anger, guilt
- pining, searching for the deceased
- sadness, depression, loneliness
- recovery, acceptance of the loss, peace

COPING WITH THE LOSS

How the general population deals with the death of a loved one was investigated in 1995 by the AMERICAN ASSOCIATION OF RETIRED PERSONS ("AARP"). AARP asked National Communications Research to conduct a telephone survey of over 5,000 people aged 40 or older. Approximately one third of the respondents reported that they had experienced the loss of a close friend or family member within the past year.

Those reporting a loss were asked to describe specific coping activities that they had engaged in since the death of their loved one.

    67% reported talking with friends and family
    16% read an article or book about how
           to cope with death
     9% received help with legal
           or practical arrangements
     5% attended a grief support group

When asked what strategies they found to be most helpful in coping with their loss:

    28% said talking with a friend or family
           member was most helpful
    24% said their religion was most helpful
    10% said knowing it was for the best
     6% said memories of the deceased
     4% reported staying busy as the best strategy.

It is interesting to note that 67% of the people who suffered a loss turned to family and friends to help them cope with the loss. Although talking with family and friends topped the list as the most commonly used strategy, only 28% reported this as being most helpful to them.

HELPING THE BEREAVED

Many times friends and family members want to help but they are at a loss as to what to say or do. The next section discusses different techniques that can be used to help with the grieving process. Family and friends want to help the person who is grieving, but sometimes they don't know how to do it. They may feel just as helpless in dealing with the loss as does the bereaved — not knowing what to say to console those grieving.

There are no magic words, but saying you are sorry for the loss is appropriate and generally well received. Avoid platitudes such as: "It was fate." "It was God's will." "It was for the best." Especially avoid telling the bereaved that you know how he/she feels.   People who suffer a great loss do not believe that anyone can understand how they feel; and they are probably correct. It is better to tell the bereaved what you are feeling:
　　"I was shocked when I heard of the death."
　　"I am so sad for you."
　　"I am going to really miss him."
 Knowing that you share the feeling of loss is comforting to someone who is grieving.

Listening is more important than talking to the bereaved. They may need to explore the circumstances of the death — how the person died; where and when he died, etc. They may need to express what they are feeling, whether it be grief or anger. Try not to change the subject just because you are uncomfortable with the topic or with the expression of emotion.

If the bereaved wishes to reminisce about the decedent, then join in the conversation. Talk about the decedent's good qualities and the enjoyable times that you shared.

If during the funeral period, you want to do something such as prepare food or send flowers, then consider asking the bereaved for permission to do so. The family may prefer donations to a favorite charity in place of flowers. The family may have already made dinner plans for the guests. Do not make general offers of assistance. "Let me know if you need anything" is not likely to get a response even if the bereaved does need help with something. A better, more sincere, approach is a specific offer, such as, "If you need transportation, I can drive you to the cemetery."

Your assistance during the post-funeral period is more important than during the funeral period. During the funeral the bereaved is usually surrounded by family and friends and has more than ample assistance. Any offer to help at that time may not even register because the bereaved may be numb with grief — unable to comprehend what is going on around them — unable to even recall who was present at the funeral, nonetheless who offered to assist them.

Once the funeral is over and everyone has gone home, that is the time to offer support. The bereaved needs to go through a transition period and must learn to live without the presence of their loved one. In general, the more dependent the bereaved was on the decedent, the more difficult the transition. In such case, you can be most helpful if you are able to offer assistance with those tasks of daily living that the bereaved is not accustomed to performing. For example, if the decedent was the sole driver in the family, then you might help the bereaved to learn to drive or at least help find public transportation. If the decedent handled all of the family finances, you might assist the bereaved in bill paying and balancing a checkbook. If math is not your forte, help to find a bookkeeper who can assist for a reasonable fee.

But, the best thing that family and friends can do for the bereaved is just to be there for them. As shown by the AARP survey, the specific coping activity used by the majority of the bereaved was to talk to a friend or relative. A telephone call, or a card on a special anniversary or holiday, will be appreciated. You can help most with a call or a visit. It is just that simple.

Also be patient with the bereaved. There is no set time to get through the grieving process.   It may take considerable time for the mourner to be able to find some quality of life.   If several months have passed and you are concerned that the bereaved is still not functioning well, or at least better, then you might consider suggesting that the bereaved seek professional counseling. Try not to be judgmental when making the suggestion. Don't say "You should be feeling better by now," but rather, "I can see that you are still having a hard time getting through this difficult period. Have you considered seeing _____"

Suggest whatever is appropriate to the mourner. For example, if the mourner is a religious person, then suggest a visit with their religious leader. If the mourner is a social person, then suggest a support group.   If the bereaved is severely depressed then a visit to a doctor or psychiatrist may be the best recommendation.

Do not expect your recommendation to be well received. The mourner may become angry or annoyed that you even made the suggestion. It may be difficult for the mourner to accept the fact that he/she needs assistance. Some people, mostly men, think it an admission of weakness to agree that they need help.   They believe they should be able to "tough it out."

Some mourners may have increased their consumption of alcohol or turned to drugs in an attempt to deal with the pain that they are experiencing. If they accept your suggestion, they may need to deal with a growing addiction in addition to the problem of overcoming the grief and they may not be willing to do that.

Elderly people might think there is a stigma associated with any kind of counseling. They may insist "There's nothing wrong with me" fearing that you think they are unbalanced or somehow mentally defective.

Some people, especially the overachiever type, refuse to seek counseling because they perceive asking for help to be a sign of failure — an admission that they failed to work out the problem themselves. It's as if they failed "Grieving 101."

But those most resistant to a suggestion of a need for counseling are mourners who use denial as a defense mechanism. They may brush off the suggestion with "No. I'm alright" or "I'm doing a lot better." If they deny that they are having trouble getting past the grief, then they do not need to deal with the problem. If they deny that they have a problem, then they don't have the problem and that solves that!

In such cases, the timeworn adage, "You can lead a horse to water, but you can't make him drink," applies. The mourner needs to take the first step himself. You cannot take it for him. All you can do is assure the mourner (and yourself) that you have confidence that he/she can, and will, work this through.

HELPING A CHILD THROUGH THE LOSS

The first thing parents observe about their second child is how very different that child is from their first child. Parents quickly learn that each of their children is an individual, with his/her own separate response to any given situation. It is important to keep this fact in mind when trying to assist a child through the loss of a close family member or friend. Because each child is different, there is no single proper way to assist a child through a period of mourning. You can help the child most if you consider the child's background as it relates to the loss:

What is the child's relationship to the decedent?
What were the circumstances of the death?
Was it expected or was it sudden or tragic?
What is the emotional age of the child? That age may differ significantly from his/her chronological age.

As an example, consider the family of Harold and Elaine, parents of three children. Emily, the eldest child, was one of those "born old" children, wise beyond her years, sensitive and shy. Her brother John, two years her junior was the direct opposite — boisterous, immature, constantly in motion. Peter came along five years later. He was the baby of the family, a cherub, always smiling, indulged by both parent and sibling.

When their paternal grandfather died, Emily was 10, John, 8 and Peter, 3. Their parents expected the death because "Gramps" had been suffering from cancer for a long time. No mention was made to the children of the serious nature of the illness, so Emily was surprised to learn of the death. She shed no tears but retreated to her room and soon became occupied with a computer game.

John and his father cried together when they were told that Gramps had died. Gramps was both kind and generous with a great sense of humor. Best of all he was never critical of John's rambunctious behavior. It seemed to John and his Dad that they lost the best friend they ever had.

Peter did not understand what was going on; but he reacted empathetically, patting John on the shoulder, and saying "Don't cry Johnny."

When it came time to go to the funeral Emily refused to go. Johnny got angry with Emily for something or another and pushed her down. She was not hurt, but she cried loudly and carried on. Peter started whining. The whole day was hard on their parents.

The next few months were equally difficult. John woke up with nightmares. Emily was sullen and withdrawn. No one mentioned the death except Peter who was full of questions: "Where's Gramps?"
"Was he in that box?"
"Where did they put the box?"
"Why was everyone crying?"

Harold and Elaine were having their own problems dealing with the loss and they had no patience with the children. The family eventually got back to normal, but it might have been easier on all of them had the parents prepared the children for the dying process.

PREPARING FOR THE EVENT

Most deaths are expected. The majority of people who die are ill for several months before their death. Children are not always aware of a family member's mortal illness so it comes as a shock to them when it happens. It might have been easier on Emily and John if their parents said something like:

> *Gramps is old and very ill. It happens that all living things, plants, animals and people, eventually die. No one knows for sure when someone will die, but it may be that because he is so old and so very sick that Gramps may die sometime within the year.*

If either child wanted to pursue the subject then that could lead to a discussion of the funeral process:

> *When someone dies in our family, all of our friends and family gather together to talk about how much we loved the person and how much we will miss having that person with us. Later we go to the gravesite where we say prayers and our last good-byes.*

It is important for parents to explain the children's role in this process, but like most couples, Harold and Elaine never thought about, much less discussed, their children's participation in the funeral and burial service. Had her parents told Emily what to expect and what was expected of her, she might not have objected to attending the funeral.

Before discussing the matter with the child, it is important that a husband and wife explore their own views on their children's participation in a funeral and burial. They may find that they have differing views on the following issues:

What factors should determine whether a child attends the wake and/or funeral:

▷ custom or convenience?

▷ the age and emotional maturity of that child?

▷ the relationship of the child to the decedent?

Should the child be allowed to decide whether he/she wishes to attend the wake and/or funeral?

Should a child be allowed (or encouraged) to touch or kiss the corpse?

Should children participate in grave site ceremonies?

Should a child be encouraged or required to visit the grave site at a later date?

There are no right or wrong answers for any of the above questions. Each family has its own set of customs and values and the answers to these questions need to conform to those customs and values. What is important is that the couple agree about what they expect of their children and then impart that expectation to their children.

The "imparting" is the difficult part. No one likes to talk about death. Parents have been told that they need to discuss sex with their children. They have been told that they need to discuss drugs with their children. These are important, life threatening, issues but it is entirely possible that a child will grow to be an adult without ever having someone close to them die. So why bring up the subject?

The reason to discuss the matter is the same reason to discuss sex with your children. The sex they see on television or hear about from their friends is a reflection of societal values but perhaps not your family values. You discuss sex to impart your family values and expectations to your children. If you wish to express to your children your views on the dying process and the afterlife (or the lack of it, if that is your belief) then it is appropriate to discuss these matters when you believe the child is sufficiently mature and ready for the discussion.

Still another reason to discuss death with the child is when someone close to them is quite aged or seriously ill. If they heard that some family member is dying, they may have concerns or questions that you can answer. Most children fear the unknown and death is an unknown to them. Of course, children are aware of the fact of death almost as soon as they can speak. It is all around them. Animated characters "die" as part of a computer game. Children's cartoon movies and television shows contain death and dying scenes. A child may have a pet that dies. Children hear about people dying almost nightly on the news.

Although children are familiar with the concept of death, they do not know how they or their family will react to the death of a loved one. If the topic is discussed prior to an impending death, the child may find it comforting to know what to expect, what behavior is expected of them, and what choices they may have regarding their attendance at a wake or funeral.

AFTER THE FUNERAL

Once the funeral is over, you need to deal with your own loss. That may be a difficult process for you so you may not even notice that your child is also grieving. This was the case with the Harold and Elaine. They were not aware that Emily was having a difficult time with the loss — after all she didn't even cry when she heard of the death. Had they thought about it, they may have realized that Emily was retreating into herself as a defense mechanism for dealing with the loss. Her continued sullen attitude after the funeral was a tip off that she was having difficulty getting beyond the loss.

If her parents had encouraged Emily to talk about the problem, they would have learned that she had ambivalent feelings about her grandfather. She loved him, but she felt that he favored her brothers. Gramps always played "boy" games of catch and touch football. He never took the time to get to know Emily and she resented that. Now that he was gone, there would be no opportunity for her to have a meaningful relationship with her grandfather.

People are helped most by talking with a friend or relative about their loss. The same applies to children. Emily would have profited had she been able to explore her feelings with either of her parents. Her parents might also have profited because they may have developed a closer relationship with Emily and established a pattern of open communication.

As it was, Emily never did resolve the problem. Her parents suffered her sullenness without ever a clue as to what Emily was all about. Unfortunately, this lack of communication continued as Emily grew older and ever more a closed book.

John fared better. Harold recognized that John's nightmares were related to the loss. Harold made an effort to spend more time with the boy and not to be so critical when John acted up.

As for Peter, his parents tried to answer his questions as best as they were able. Elaine had the uneasy feeling that she was not answering them "the right way." She thought she made a mistake by saying that "Gramps is now at rest" because Peter asked if Gramps was sleeping. She thought that she might have caused Peter to confuse death and sleep.

Had Elaine investigated she could have found any number of excellent publications dealing with the subject. Many funeral homes provide families with complimentary pamphlets on how to answer children's questions about death. The local library and bookstore have any number of excellent publications designed to answer questions raised by small children.

Most religious organizations offer printed material for young people that explain death from the organization's perspective. For religious families, this is a good opportunity for the family to discuss their religious beliefs as they relate to the loss of a loved one.

INTERNET RESOURCES

Many Web sites offer free publications on how to deal with the issues of death and dying. You can use your browser to locate such sites.

Today's child is computer literate. A child may, on his own, decide to seek an E-mail buddy to work through a problem the child may be having with the death. Parents need to supervise such communication because the child may be especially vulnerable at this point in his/her life.

There are Web sites that offer organized E-mail grief support groups. One such site is GriefNet. This Web site is operated by Rivendell Resources, a nonprofit organization:

GriefNet   1- 734-761-1960
P.O. Box 3272
Ann Arbor, MI 48106-3272
          E-mail: visibility@griefnet.org

KIDSAID is a companion Web site to GriefNet. They offer peer support groups for children who are dealing with a loss.   Parental permission is required before the child is allowed to join a support group.

http://www.griefnet.org/KIDSAID/kids2kids.html

THE TROUBLED CHILD

Most deaths are from natural causes. The death is expected and not all that difficult for the family to finally accept. The *problem death* is one that is tragic, unexpected, and/or a death that cuts short a life. More and more school officials are recognizing that the loss of a member of the school community deeply affects the student population. Many schools have adopted a policy of having school psychologists counsel the children as soon as the death occurs. They do not wait until a school child shows signs of being disturbed by the event.

It would be well for parents to adopt the same policy. Specifically, if your family suffers a problem death then consider seeking the services of a professional who is experienced in grief counseling just as soon after the death as is practicable.

A death does not always need to be a problem death to cause a problem in a child. As discussed before, if a child has unresolved issues, then that child may need professional assistance in coping with the loss. Children do not manifest grief or depression in the same way as adults, so look for changes that are atypical of the child and that do not resolve themselves within a reasonable time after the death. Consider consulting with a child psychologist if your child exhibits unusual or antisocial behavior such as:

- eating too much or too little
- destructive or aggressive behavior
- sleeping too much or too little
- sudden change in school performance
- misbehavior at school

The red flag, signaling an immediate need for counseling, is a child who talks or writes about committing suicide. It is important to act quickly to show the child that you understand that he/she is having a rough time and that you and the doctor are going to assist the child with the problem.

There are any number of resources in the community to assist the child, from school counselors to religious organizations. The NEW YORK STATE PSYCHOLOGICAL ASSOCIATION, located in Albany, can refer you to a psychologist in your geographic area who is experienced in grief counseling. You can reach them at (800) 445-0899.

For those who cannot afford private care, counties offer low-cost services on an ability to pay basis. Some religious organizations offer counseling services to their members, as well as to the general public, on a sliding scale basis.

Before seeking counseling services, it is important to schedule a physical checkup for the child. There is a chance that the problem is physiological. Some illnesses cause behavioral changes; for example, food allergies can cause aggressive behavior. Hearing or visual deficiencies can cause a child to withdraw into himself. Even infections can cause behavioral disturbances. Perhaps the child is on drugs and an examination should pick that up. All these things need to be ruled out prior to counseling.

If your child has been treated by the physician over the years, the doctor may know the child well enough to be able to offer some insight into the problem. If the checkup does not reveal a physical problem, the physician may be able to suggest the right type of treatment, i.e., psychologist or psychiatrist, and perhaps give you a referral.

CHOOSING THE RIGHT COUNSELOR

There was a film called GOODWILL HUNTING in which a brilliant, but troubled, teenager was required, by court order, to attend counseling. The funniest part of the film was the manner in which the boy went through counselors. He deliberately alienated (and was alienated) by many doctors until he met the right one for him. Similarly, if your child needs counseling you might need to interview several counselors before you find someone with whom your child can work; someone who speaks on his/her level — someone the child can trust.

The issue of trust may create a dilemma for the parent. The child is the counselor's patient. The counselor cannot betray the child's trust by revealing what was said during treatment, yet parents need to know whether the treatment is helping the child. The counselor can, and should, disclose to the parent the diagnosis, prognosis and type of proposed treatment. The parents need to employ someone they trust to pursue the course of treatment that they have determined is best for their child.

In seeking a counselor, personal references are the best avenue, although it may be difficult to find a friend or relation who has had his/her child successfully treated for a similar problem.   With or without references, you need to investigate the counselor's background. What is his/her training? What percentage of the practice is devoted to children in this age group?   Is the counselor experienced in working with children who are having difficulty coping with the loss of a loved one?

Interview more than one counselor before making your choice. If the child is sufficiently mature and able to cooperate in choosing the right counselor, then that is an important step forward. If not, you may need to be assertive and go with the counselor whom you trust and are most comfortable. If it turns out that there is no improvement within a few months, then you need to find another counselor.   As with the student in GOODWILL HUNTING, it may take several tries before you come upon someone who can help your child.

STRATEGIES TO COPE WITH THE LOSS

Once the person accepts the fact of death, they are past the initial phase of the grief process. Most people do very well and are able to go through the remaining stages with no overt effort on their part. Others suffer profoundly and need to find ways to get through the grieving process. If you have recently experienced a loss and are having difficulty coping with the loss then consider your own personality type and explore those strategies that might help you through.

Do you enjoy socializing with people or do you prefer solitary activities? Are you a "do-it-yourself" type of person or do you feel more at ease with someone leading you through the process?

STRATEGIES FOR THE PRIVATE PERSON

If you find socializing to be difficult, then consider non-social activities such as reading a self help book. There are many excellent publications that explore the grieving process and how to adjust to the loss. Praying or quiet meditation may offer you consolation. This may be a good time to explore different kinds of meditative techniques. You can find books on meditative techniques such as Zen or visualization in the Philosophy section of the library or bookstore. You can find books on Yoga in the exercise section.

If you are computer literate, then you can use your browser to locate an Internet support group. An anonymous friend may be the perfect confidant to help you to work through the sadness and loneliness that you are feeling. You can locate E-mail support groups for people who are dealing with all types of grief issues by searching the following topics: GRIEF   MOURNING   DEATH   DYING

STRATEGIES FOR THE SOCIAL MINDED

If you are a social person, then consider using those types of activities that involve a social setting, such as joining a bridge, bowling or golfing group. If your grief is too deep to concentrate on recreational activities, consider joining a support group. The power of the support group is companionship. They offer the one thing you may need most at this time — just someone to listen.

If you belong to an organized religion or a civic organization, find out whether they have a support group for people who are going through a grieving process. If your organization does not have a support group, then consider starting one yourself. It can be as simple as putting a notice in a weekly bulletin that you are holding a meeting for anyone who lost a loved one within the past year. You can hold the meeting as part of a picnic or barbecue with everyone bringing a dish for others to share. Just getting together and sharing experiences may help you and others in your organization as well.

If you do not belong to an organization, then look in the newspaper for notices of meetings of local support groups or consider joining one of the many national support groups. The following are some of the well established national groups:

FOR WIDOWED PERSONS

THEOS   1-412-471-7779
(They Help Each Other Spiritually)
322 Boulevard of the Allies, Suite 105
Pittsburgh, PA 15222-1919

THEOS is a national organization with a volunteer network of recently widowed persons. They have support chapters in some 17 states. If you wish to establish a support group in your area, they will help you to do so.

☙☙☙☙☙☙☙☙☙☙☙☙☙☙☙☙☙☙☙☙☙☙☙☙☙☙☙☙☙☙☙☙

AARP GRIEF AND LOSS PROGRAM
WIDOWED PERSONS SERVICE   1-800-424-3410
601 E Street NW
Washington, DC 20049

AARP currently has support groups for widowed persons in New York. They also have support groups for adults who have suffered the loss of a family member such as a parent or sibling. Call the above number and they will refer you to the support group nearest you.

    E-mail: griefandloss@ aarp.org
         Web site: www.aarp.org/griefandloss

FOR WIDOWED PARENTS

PARENTS WITHOUT PARTNERS   1-800-637-7974
401 N. Michigan Avenue
Chicago, IL   60611-6267

PARENTS WITHOUT PARTNERS is a national nonprofit organization for single parents. They offer group discussions and single parent activities such as picnics and hikes. They have some 20 chapters throughout the state of New York. You can call the above number for the chapter nearest you — or you can check out their Web site:

 Web Site: http://parentswithoutpartners.org
E-mail: pwp@sba.com

PET GRIEF SUPPORT SERVICES

Those who suffer the loss of a pet may experience a sense of loss similar to the loss of a close family member.   Often they hesitate to turn to friends or family members (especially if they never owned a pet) believing they just wouldn't understand.

Most local Humane Societies and some Schools of Veterinary medicine offer pet loss counseling.

 There is a list of pet grief counseling services for New York and other states at
http://www.superdog.com/petloss/

BE GOOD TO YOU

People who suffer extreme grief tend to become extreme in everyday activities. They may forget to eat. Some find themselves eating all day. Some mourners develop sleep disturbances and go without sleep for long periods of time while others suffer the opposite extreme of wanting to sleep all day. If you find that your grief is affecting your physical well being, then you need to make a conscious effort to take care of yourself:

✴ EAT A BALANCED NUTRITIONAL DIET

Contrary to popular taste, sugar, salt, fat and chocolate do not constitute the four basic food groups. And contrary to current food faddism, no one diet fits all. The ability to digest certain foods varies from person to person and we all have ethnic preferences. You need to learn what balance of fats, protein (meat, fish, legumes) and carbohydrates (fruit, vegetables, grains) you require to maintain your optimum weight and state of well being; and then make an effort to keep that balance in your daily diet.

✴ GET SUFFICIENT REST

There is much variation in the amount of sleep required from person to person. You know how much sleep you normally require. Try to maintain your usual, pre-loss, sleep pattern. If you are finding difficulty sleeping at night, resist the urge to sleep during the day. It is easy to reverse your days and nights. Awake all night, dozing all day, will only make you feel as if you are walking around in a fog.

✴ EXERCISE EACH DAY

Exercise can be as simple as taking a brisk 20 minute walk, however the more sustained and energetic, the greater the benefit. If you are having trouble sleeping at night, try exercising during the late afternoon and eating your main meal at lunch rather than late at night.

✴ THINK POSITIVE THOUGHTS

Make an effort to concentrate on things in your life that are right, as opposed to thoughts that make you angry or sad. This may be difficult to do. During periods of high stress, you may feel as if your mind has a mind of its own. Thoughts may race through your mind even though you'd just as soon not think them. Prayer and/or meditation may help you to reestablish discipline in your thinking process.

Eating right, getting sufficient sleep, exercising and thinking positive thoughts — most people have heard these recommendations from so many sources (doctors, psychologists, writers for health magazines, etc.) that they seem to have become a cliche. But the reason that so many professionals make these suggestions is simply that they work. Doing all these things will make you feel significantly better.

But if you feel so down that you are unable to help yourself, then you may need professional help to get you through this difficult period. Check with your health care plan to see if they will cover the cost of a visit to a psychiatrist or psychologist.

ADJUSTING TO A NEW LIFE STYLE

If you lost a member of your immediate family, then in addition to going through the stages of the grieving process, you need to go through a transition period in which you learn how to live without the decedent. The child must learn to live without the guidance of a parent. Parents may need to put their parenting behind them. The spouse must learn to live without a partner, and as a single person.

In addition to learning to live with the loss, the bereaved may need to establish a new identity. Such was the case with Claire. She and Fred were married 44 years when he died after a lengthy battle with cancer. At first Claire didn't think she could live without him. She had been a wife for so long. She had trouble thinking of herself as a single person — nonetheless being one.

Claire had difficulty accepting the fact that Fred was dead, even though she expected he would die for months before he did. She would see Fred in her dreams. Sometimes she thought she saw him sitting in his favorite chair. When Fred appeared to Claire, he looked the same as when they were first married. Sometimes she thought he was speaking to her.

What was most comforting to Claire was that Fred was smiling at her. She was relieved to know that Fred was no longer in pain and was at peace. The smile on his face was a relief to her because she feared he might be angry with her for the many times he would call out her name and she would become annoyed with him. She felt guilty that she did not have more patience as a caregiver.

Claire found herself talking to Fred especially during those times that she was undecided as to what to do. As time progressed, she began to incorporate her husband's beliefs into her own so that instead of asking herself "What should I do?" it became "This is what Fred would have done."

Eventually Claire found that she was able to function on her own. She began to reengage with the world. She found new interests to pleasantly occupy her time. She learned how to live as a single person. She is now more self sufficient than at any other time in her life. She laments that Fred no longer visits her. She still misses him.

Claire was able to get beyond the grief. She did it on her own, though she will tell you that she did it with Fred's help.

Claire's case is not unusual. As verified by the AARP survey, most people adjust to the loss on their own, requiring only an assist from family and friends, but there is a percentage of the grieving population that will require assistance and may need professional grief counseling.

For those experiencing psychological problems prior to the death, the event of the death may be the precipitating factor to mental illness requiring treatment. If a person had a drinking problem or a drug addiction before the death, the event of the death may exacerbate the addiction. Some deaths are so violent or tragic, that even the sturdiest may be unable to resume their life without professional assistance. In the next section, we discuss ways of coping with the problem death.

THE PROBLEM DEATH

We described the problem death is one that is unexpected, tragic or a death that cuts short a life. Such a death is a often an immediate problem in terms of the funeral, burial and estate settlement, but the more difficult problem is getting through the mourning period.

The death of a child is always a problem death. Even if the child is an adult, the parent experiences extreme grief. No one expects to outlive his or her child. In these days of a lengthening life cycle, more and more parents may come to experience such a loss. The loss may come at a time when the parent is frail or in poor health, making it all the more difficult to deal with the loss.

The only thing harder than losing an adult child is losing a young child. Nothing compares to the intensity of grief experienced by a parent when a little one dies. Some parents believe they are losing their mind. Many feel that their lives can never have meaning again. Guilt and recrimination flow, "Maybe I could have prevented it." There is even guilt for returning to ordinary living. If the parents find themselves smiling, laughing or making love they think, "How can we be doing this? How can we ever be normal again?"

The family who experiences a tragic or violent death should consider seeking professional grief counseling as soon as practicable after the death. The grief counseling can be in the format of a self-help group. Participants are able to talk and share their pain with others like themselves who understand what they are experiencing.

There are many specialized self-help groups that provide literature and peer support for families who experience a problem death.

FOR PRENATAL OR NEONATAL DEATHS

M.E.N.D. **M**ommies **E**nduring **N**eonatal **D**eath
P.O. Box 1007   1-888-695-MEND
Coppell, TX   75019

MEND has a Web site and provides monthly newsletters.

  http://www.mend.org
  E-mail   rebekah@mend.org

☙☙☙☙☙☙☙☙☙☙☙☙☙☙☙☙☙☙☙☙☙☙☙☙☙☙☙☙☙☙☙☙☙☙☙

SHARE   1-800-821-6819
National Share Pregnancy and Infant Loss Support
St. Joseph Health Center
300 First Corporate Drive
St. Charles, MO   63012-2893

SHARE has support groups throughout the United States. You can call the national office for the telephone number of the support group in New York.

  http://www.nationalshareoffice.com
  E-mail   share@nationalshareoffice

FOR FAMILIES OF A DECEASED CHILD

THE COMPASSIONATE FRIENDS
National Chapter: 1-630-990-0010
P.O. Box 3696, Oak Brook, IL 60522
THE COMPASSIONATE FRIENDS have 23 chapters in New York with volunteers (themselves bereaved parents) to accept telephone calls.

http://www.compassionatefriends.org
E-mail tcf_national@prodigy.com

ᏋᏋᏋᏋᏋᏋᏋᏋᏋᏋᏋᏋᏋᏋᏋᏋᏋᏋᏋᏋᏋᏋᏋᏋᏋᏋᏋᏋᏋᏋᏋᏋ

A.G.A.S.T   1-888-774-7437
ALLIANCE OF GRANDPARENTS A SUPPORT IN TRAGEDY
P.O. Box 17281
Phoenix, AZ 85011-0281
AGAST supports grandparents, who have suffered the loss of a grandchild, with informational packets, peer contact and newsletters.

E-mail: GRANMASIDS@AOL.COM

ᏋᏋᏋᏋᏋᏋᏋᏋᏋᏋᏋᏋᏋᏋᏋᏋᏋᏋᏋᏋᏋᏋᏋᏋᏋᏋᏋᏋᏋᏋᏋᏋ

THE SIDS ALLIANCE   1-800-221-7437
1314 Bedford Ave.; Suite 210
Baltimore, MD 21208
The Sudden Infant Death Syndrome Allianceis a national, not-for-profit, organization dedicated to the support of SIDS families, education and research. They have offices in Buffalo, Rochester, Albany, Deer Park (Long Island) and Walker Valley.

http://www.sidsalliance.org/
E-mail: ncsids@webcom.com

FOR FAMILIES OF MURDERED CHILDREN

THE NATIONAL ORGANIZATION OF   (888) 818-POMC
PARENTS **O**F **M**URDERED **C**HILDREN, INC.
National Chapter
100 East Eighth Street, B-41
Cincinnati, OH   45202

POMC has support groups and contact people in each
of the fifty states.   Contact the National Chapter for the
telephone number of the group nearest you.

http://www.pomc.org
E-mail   natlpomc@aol.com

FOR FAMILIES OF SUICIDES

AMERICAN ASSOC. OF SUICIDOLOGY   (202) 237-2280
4201 Connecticut Ave., NW Suite 408
Washington, DC 20008

The American Association of Suicidology is a non-profit
organization that offers newsletters and information
about support groups throughout the United States.
They can refer you to different organizations in the state
of New York that seek to prevent suicide and to provide
support groups for families who have suffered a loss
through suicide. Call the above number for the support
group nearest you.

http://www.suicidology.org/survivorsupport.htm

BUT WHAT IF I CAN'T STOP GRIEVING?

We observed that there are five stages of grieving:
shock/disbelief,
anger/guilt
searching/pining
sadness/depression
acceptance of the loss.

There is no right way to grieve. You may pass through a stage rapidly or even skip a stage. You may get hung up in one of the stages and have difficulty getting beyond that emotion. Some psychologists refer to this as "stuckness." It's something like what happened to 45-rpm phonograph records that were popular in the 1940's and 1950's. For the benefit of the digital generation who have no experience with phonographs, the record was played by means of a needle that glided over groves of a revolving disk (the record). Sometimes the needle would get stuck in a groove and play the same sound over and over again until the annoyed listener bumped it into the next groove.

If you are stuck in one of the stages of mourning you may think the suggestions in this section to be useless in your situation because they encourage you to be proactive, i.e., to actively seek to help yourself. If you are thinking:
"I **can't** help myself. " or
"If I could help myself, I wouldn't have this problem," then the first thing you need to understand, and accept, is that you have no other choice but to help yourself. The pain exists within you and no where else. Because the pain is internal and unique to you, only you can ease that pain. This does not mean that no one can help you to deal with the pain. It just means that you need to be interactive with the healing process; and in particular, you need to take the first step.

What is that first step? To answer that question you need to identify those areas of your life with which you are having difficulty. It might help to make a list of all of the things that are bothering you. Once you compose the list, look at the last item on the list. If you are like most people, you will initially avoid thinking about what is really troubling you. It may take the last item on the list for you to admit to yourself what is really causing the problem.

Once you identify the problem, the identification itself should suggest the solution. For example, suppose you find the holidays unbearable, then a solution may be to change your holiday routine. Instead of wearing yourself out shopping for gifts, use the money to treat yourself to a boat cruise. Tell everyone that this year you are taking a holiday from the holidays. You may find that people are just as tired of exchanging gifts as you are and that they gladly welcome the change.

If your problem is being lonely, then your solution will involve companionship. How you attain that companionship will depend on your personality. If you are lonely, but not a social person, consider adopting a pet. If you are civic minded, then you may find companionship as a volunteer for community activities. If you are physically active, then perhaps you can take up a new sport or even pick up a sport that you used to enjoy at an earlier time in your life. If you enjoy sports but are not in the best shape, perhaps you can coach children's team sports.

If your problem is that you are severely depressed, then the solution will involve medical and/or psychological methods of lifting the depression. If you decide to ask for medical assistance, you need to continue to be interactive. You cannot stand passively by saying "Now heal me." Pharmaceutical hyperbole notwithstanding, there is no magic pill. An antidepressant may help you to gain control of yourself, but you still need to work through the grief.

If you feel that you have tried it all and you still are unable to find peace and contentment in your life, then you need to ask the hard question:
"What is it about mourning that I really enjoy?"
Strange question? Not really.

You may enjoy thinking of your loved one even if the thought gives you as much pain as pleasure. You may think that if you stop mourning then you truly lose the decedent. If that's the case, then compartmentalize your grief, that is, set aside a special time of the day to actively think about and/or grieve for your loved one and the rest of the day not to grieve or even think about the decedent.

Actively plan the grieving compartment of your day. You may wish to have a grieving routine, perhaps visit the grave site once a week; or quietly spend 15 minutes a day looking at pictures of the decedent or writing down your memories of the happy times you had together. If you have been discussing your grief with family or friends, restrict such talks to specific times, perhaps on the decedent's birthday, or on the anniversary of his death.

Set aside as much time each day as you believe you need to mourn, but here is the hard part — you need to exercise self restraint not to mourn, nor talk about, nor even think of the decedent during any other part of the day. If your mind wanders back to the sadness and loneliness of the loss, postpone it. Say to yourself, "Hold that thought till my next grieving compartment."

If you are speaking to someone, do not mention the decedent or how you are feeling about the loss until your scheduled grieving talk with that person. If the subject comes up during a conversation, then change the subject by saying "We'll talk about that later."

Hopefully you will find the pain of your loss to lessen over time, in frequency and/or intensity. It isn't so much that time heals; it is more that you learn to heal yourself over time.

Glossary

ADMINISTRATION The *administration* of a Probate Estate is the management and settlement of the decedent's affairs under the supervision of a probate court.

AFFIANT   An *affiant* is someone who signs an affidavit and swears that it is true in the presence of the notary public or person with authority to administer an oath.

AFFIDAVIT   An *affidavit* is a written statement of fact made by someone voluntarily and under oath, in the presence of a notary public or someone who has authority to administer an oath.

ANATOMICAL GIFT   An *anatomical gift* is the donation of all or part of the body of the decedent for a specified purpose, such as transplantation or research.

ANCILLARY An *ancillary* probate procedure is a secondary probate proceeding that aids or assists the original probate proceeding. Ancillary probate proceedings are held in another state for the purpose of determining the beneficiary of property located in that state.

ANNUITANT   An *annuitant* is someone who is entitled to receive payments under an annuity contract.

ANNUITY   An *annuity* is the right to receive fixed, periodic payments either for life or for a number of years.

ASSET An *asset* is anything owned by someone that has a value, including personal property (jewelry, paintings, securities, cash, motor vehicles, etc.) and real property (condominiums, vacant lots, acreage, residences, etc.)

BENEFICIARY A *beneficiary* is one who benefits from the acts of another person, such as someone who inherits property from the decedent.

CLAIM A *claim* against the decedent's estate is a demand for payment. To be effective, the claim must be filed with the appropriate court within the time limits set by law.

CODICIL A *codicil* to a Will is a supplement or an addition to a Will that changes certain parts of the Will.

COLUMBARIUM A *columbarium* is a vault with niches (spaces) for urns that contain the ashes of cremated bodies.

COMMUNITY PROPERTY Certain states (Arizona, California, Idaho, Louisiana, Nevada, New Mexico, Texas, Washington, Wisconsin) have laws stating that property acquired by husband or wife, or both, during their marriage is *community property* and is owned equally by both of them. (See separate property.)

CREMAINS The word *cremains* is an abbreviation of the term *cremated remains*. It is also referred to as the cremated person's *ashes.*

DECEDENT The *decedent* is the person who died.

DESCENDANT A *descendant* of the decedent is someone from a later generation, such as the decedent's child, grandchild, great-grandchild. The New York Rules of Intestate Succession include adopted children as a descendant of the decedent. The word *issue* has the same legal meaning as the word *descendant*.

DISTRIBUTION The *distribution* of a trust estate or of a Probate Estate is the giving to the beneficiary that part of the estate to which the beneficiary is entitled.

ESTATE A person's *estate* is all of the property (both real and personal property) owned by that person. A person's estate is also referred to as his *taxable estate* because all of the decedent's assets must be included when determining whether any estate taxes are due when the person dies.

EXECUTOR An *executor* is someone that a person appointed by the maker of a Will to carry out the directions that the maker gives in his Will.

FIDUCIARY A *fiduciary* is one who holds property in trust for another or one who acts for the benefit of another.

GRANTEE The *grantee* (also called the party of the second part) named in a deed is the person who receives title to the property from the grantor.

GRANTOR A *grantor* is someone who transfers property. The grantor, also called the party of the first part, named in a deed, is the person who is transferring the property to the new owner (the *grantee*). The grantor of a trust is someone who creates the trust and then transfers property into the trust. See *settlor*.

HEALTH CARE AGENT A *Health Care Agent* is a person appointed by someone (the *Principal*) in a Health Care Proxy to make to make medical decisions for the Principal in the event he is too ill to make his own decisions.

HEIR   An *heir* is someone who is entitled to inherit the decedent's property in the event that the decedent dies intestate (without a Will). This includes the surviving spouse and the state of New York as heir of last resort, if the descendant had no surviving relatives.

HOMESTEAD   A person's *homestead* is the dwelling and land, owned and occupied, by that person as his principal residence. The definition of homestead includes condominiums, cooperatives, and mobile homes.

INDIGENT   An person who is *indigent* is a person who is poor, destitute and without funds.

ISSUE   An *issue* of the decedent is a lineal descendant of the decedent.

INTESTATE   *Intestate* means not having a Will or dying without a Will. *Testate* is to have a Will or dying with a Will.

IRREVOCABLE CONTRACT   An *irrevocable* contract is a contract that cannot be revoked, withdrawn, or cancelled by any of the parties to that contract.

JOINT AND SEVERAL LIABILITY If two or more people have *joint and several liabiltiy,* this means that they all together are responsible to pay the debt and each one of them individually is also responsible to pay the debt.

KEY MAN INSURANCE   *Key man insurance* is an insurance policy designed to protect a company from economic loss in the event that an important employee of the company becomes disabled or dies.

LEGALESE   *Legalese* is the special vocabulary used by attorneys to draft legal documents.

LETTERS *Letters* is the term given to a document, issued by the Surrogate's court, giving someone authority to administer the estate of the decedent.

LIFE ESTATE A *life estate* interest in real property is the right to possess and occupy that property for so long as the holder of the life estate lives.

LITIGATION *Litigation* is the process of carrying on a lawsuit, i.e., to sue for some right or remedy in a court of law.

LIVING WILL A *Living Will* is a written, witnessed statement, stating whether the person who signs the Living Will wishes life support systems to be applied in the event that person is terminally ill.

MEDICAID *Medicaid* is a public assistance program sponsored jointly by the federal and state government to provide medical care for people with low income.

NEXT OF KIN *Next of kin* can refer to a person's nearest blood relation or it can refer to those people (not necessarily blood relations) who are entitled to inherit the property of the decedent if the decedent died without a will.

PERJURY *Perjury* is lying under oath. The false statement can be made as a witness in court or by signing an Affidavit. Perjury is a criminal offense.

PERSONAL PROPERTY *Personal property* is all property owned by a person that is not real property (real estate). It includes cars, stocks, house furnishings, jewelry, etc. Personal property is sometimes called *personalty*.

PERSONAL REPRESENTATIVE   A *Personal Representative* is someone appointed by the Surrogate's court to settle the decedent's estate and to distribute whatever is left to the proper beneficiary.

PER STIRPES GIFT   A *per stirpes* gift is a gift which is given to a group of people such that if one of them dies before the gift is given, then that deceased person's share goes to his/her lineal descendants.

POST-NUPTIAL AGREEMENT   A *post-nuptial agreement* is an agreement made by a couple after marriage to decide their respective rights in case of a dissolution or death of a spouse.

PRE-NUPTIAL AGREEMENT   A *pre-nuptial agreement* (also known as an *antenuptial agreement*) is an agreement made prior to marriage whereby a couple determines how their property is to be managed during their marriage and how their property is to be divided should one die, or they later divorce.

PROBATE   *Probate* is a court procedure in which a court (in New York, the Surrogate's court) determines whether the decedent left a valid Will and then appoints someone settle the affairs of the decedent and distribute whatever property is left to the proper beneficiary.

PROBATE ESTATE   The *Probate Estate* is that part of the decedent's estate that is subject to probate. It includes property that the decedent owned in his name only. It does not include property that was jointly or "in trust for another."

REAL PROPERTY   *Real property,* also known as *real estate,* is land and anything that is permanently attached to the land such as buildings and fences.

RESIDUARY BENEFICIARY   A *residuary beneficiary* is a beneficiary named in a Will who is to receive his share of whatever is left of the Probate Estate once gifts specified in the Will are made and all the decedent's bills, taxes and costs of probate are paid.

RESIDUARY ESTATE A *residuary estate* is that part of a probate estate that is left after all expenses and costs of administration have been paid and specific gifts have been made.

SECURED DEBT   A *secured debt* is one that is backed by some item that the creditor (lender) can take should the debtor (the borrower) default in his payment. For example, a car loan is a secured debt because the lender can take the car if the borrower does not make his payments.

SETTLOR   A *settlor* is someone who furnishes property that is placed in a trust. If the settlor is also the creator of the trust, then the settlor is also referred to as the grantor.

STATUTE OF LIMITATION A *statute of limitation* is a federal or state law that sets maximum time periods for taking legal action for a given matter. Once the time set out in the statute passes, no legal action can be taken on that matter.

SURROGATE   A *surrogate* is one who is substituted for another. In New York, the *Surrogate Court* is the name of the court that handles Probate matters.

TENANCY BY THE ENTIRETY   A *Tenancy by the Entirety* is the name of property that is held by husband and wife. It has the same legal effect as a Joint Tenancy with rights of survivorship.

TENANCY IN COMMON   *Tenancy in common* is a form of ownership such that each tenant owns his/her share without any claim to that share by the other tenants. Once a tenant in common dies, his/her share belongs to the tenant's estate and not to the remaining owners of the property.

TESTATE   *Testate* means having a Will or dying with a Will.

TITLE INSURANCE   *Title Insurance* is a policy issued by a title company after searching title to a parcel of real property.   The policy insures the accuracy of its search against any claim of a defective title.

TRUST AGREEMENT A *trust agreement* is document in which someone (the Grantor or Settlor) creates a trust and appoints a trustee to manage property placed into the trust. The usual purpose of the trust is to benefit persons or charities named by the Grantor as beneficiaries of the trust.

TRUSTEE   A *trustee* is a person, or institution, who accepts the duty of caring for property for the benefit of another.

UNDUE INFLUENCE   *Undue influence* is pressure or persuasion that overpowers a person's free will so that the dominated person is not acting intelligently or voluntarily.

UNSECURED DEBT   An *unsecured debt* is a debt based solely on the debtor's promise to pay for monies owed (see Secured Debt)

WAIVER   A *waiver* is the intentional and voluntary giving up of a known right.

INDEX

A

B

STATUTES, NEW YORK (cont.)

W

109 New York Statutes are referenced in
When Someone Dies In New York

Each state has its own set of laws relating to the settlement of a person's estate. The New York laws that are referenced in this book are very different from the laws of any other state. The author is in now in the process of "translating" *When Someone Dies . . .* for the rest of the states; that is, to write a book that incorporates the laws of the state into a book that describes how to settle the affairs of a decedent in that state. Arizona, California, Florida, Illinois and New York are in print. The printing schedule for other states are as follows:

June 2000:   Ohio, Texas and Pennsylvania
August 2000: Michigan, New Jersey, and the Carolinas

The following books are scheduled for release by the fall of the year 2000:

> *When Someone Dies in Alabama*
> *When Someone Dies In Georgia*
> *When Someone Dies In Indiana*
> *When Someone Dies In Maryland*
> *When Someone Dies In Massachusetts*
> *When Someone Dies In Minnesota*
> *When Someone Dies In Mississippi*
> *When Someone Dies In Tennessee*
> *When Someone Dies In The Virginias*
> *When Someone Dies In Washington*

To check for availability or to order any of these books call (800) 824-0823.

BOOK ORDER

MAIL ORDER: EAGLE PUBLISHING COMPANY OF BOCA
4199 N. DIXIE HWY. #2 BOCA RATON, FL 33431
TELEPHONE ORDER (800) 824-0823 FAX ORDER: (561) 338-0823
INTERNET ORDER: www.eaglepublishing.com

SHIP TO: NAME _____

ADDRESS: _____

METHOD OF PAYMENT: CHECK ☐

☐ VISA   ☐ MASTER CARD   ☐ DISCOVER   ☐ AMER. EXP.

[ ][ ][ ][ ] [ ][ ][ ][ ] [ ][ ][ ][ ] [ ][ ][ ][ ]

EXPIRATION DATE _____

PAPER BACK $25   HARD COVER $32
(Price includes shipping and handling)

	QUANTITY	AMOUNT
When Someone Dies In Alabama		
When Someone Dies In Arizona		
When Someone Dies in California		
When Someone Dies In Florida		
When Someone Dies In Georgia		
When Someone Dies In Illinois		
When Someone Dies In Indiana		
When Someone Dies In Maryland		
When Someone Dies In Massachusetts		
When Someone Dies In Michigan		
When Someone Dies In Minnesota		
When Someone Dies In Mississippi		
When Someone Dies In New Jersey		
When Someone Dies In New York		
When Someone Dies In Ohio		
When Someone Dies In Pennsylvania		
When Someone Dies In Tennessee		
When Someone Dies In Texas		
When Someone Dies In The Carolinas		
When Someone Dies in The Virginias		
When Someone Dies in Washington		
TOTAL		

When Someone Dies In New York